4.00

JOSEPH
THE JUST MAN

BY
ROSALIE MARIE LEVY

ST. PAUL EDITIONS

NIHIL OBSTAT:

    Stanislaus J. Brzana, S.T.D.
    Censor Librorum

IMPRIMATUR:

    † Josephus Aloisius
    Episcopus Buffalensis

Die 26 Novembris, 1954

ISBN 0-8198-3901-9 (cloth)
ISBN 0-8198-3902-7 (paper)

Library of Congress Catalog Card Number: 59-23942

COPYRIGHT, 1955 by the *Daughters of St. Paul*
───────────────────────────────
Printed in U.S.A. by the *Daughters of St. Paul*
50 St. Paul's Ave., Jamaica Plain, Boston, Mass. 02130

To
Saint Joseph
Illustrious Scion of David
Chosen by God
Guardian of Mary Pure
Watchful Defender of Jesus

CONTENTS

PART I

	PAGE
LIFE OF ST. JOSEPH	10

PART II

DEVOTION TO ST. JOSEPH	88
St. Joseph, Patron of Canada	92
St. Joseph and Humble Brother Andre	99
St. Joseph, a Guardian Angel	105
St. Joseph's Home, now at Loreto	111

PART III

IN PRAISE OF ST. JOSEPH	118

PART IV

LEGENDS OF ST. JOSEPH	192
FAVORS TO HIS DEVOTED CLIENTS	199

PART V

PRAYERS TO ST. JOSEPH	228

PART I

Joseph, the Just Man

In a sermon on the great Patriarch Saint Joseph, who is to be the subject of this book, Saint Bernardine of Siena spoke the following words:

"It is a general rule covering all special favors conferred upon any rational creature, that whenever Divine Providence chooses anyone for some particular grace or for some high station, It likewise bestows on the person so chosen all the gifts necessary for that high station and furnishes them abundantly. This was certified in a marked degree in Saint Joseph, the supposed father of our Lord Jesus Christ, and the true spouse of the Queen of the world and Mistress of the Angels; who was chosen by the Eternal Father as the faithful provider and guardian of His dearest treasures, that is to say, of His own Son, and of Saint Joseph's Spouse".

Having been chosen by God before all ages to assist in the work of man's Redemption, it was just that St. Joseph should become an object of special love on the part of the Almighty. His divinely appointed office in connection with the mystery of the Incarnation of the Savior of the world was, by his presence, "to cover, as with a chaste veil, the supernatural conception of the Son of God from the eyes of an unbelieving and material world".

St. Joseph was of the royal family of David — the family from which, according to the prophecies relating to the matter, the Redeemer of Mankind was to arise. A study of the genealogies as found in the Gospels of the Evangelists, St. Matthew and St. Luke, leave no doubt that the prophecies regarding the Savior of the World were fulfilled.

St. Matthew (1: 1-17) starting with Adam leads to David and thence through the generations to Joseph, "the husband of Mary, of whom was born Jesus, Who is called Christ". On the other hand St. Luke, after relating the baptism of Jesus in the Jordan, the descent of the Holy Ghost and the Voice of the Heavenly Father declaring "Thou art My beloved Son," states (3: 23-38): "Jesus was beginning about the age of thirty years: being (as it was supposed) the son of Joseph". St. Luke then ascends from Joseph, the husband of the Virgin Mary, to David, to Abraham, to Adam, "who was of God".

Readers of the genealogies may be puzzled by differences in the names of the fore-bearers leading from Adam, through David, to Joseph, and those ascending from Joseph, through David, to Adam "and God". To allay this puzzlement it may serve well to quote the great St. Augustine, in his homily on the "genealogy" as found in St. Luke.

"It is evident that the words which he (St. Luke 3: 21-23) used: 'Being, as was supposed, the son of Joseph'; were used on account of those who thought He was begotten by Joseph as other men are begotten. But if any are troubled because Matthew gives one line of ancestors, descending from David to Joseph, and Luke another, ascending from Joseph to David; it is easy when they consider that Joseph could have had two fathers: one by whom he was begotten; the other by whom he was adopted. Of old, adoption was customary among that people of God, that they might have sons, though not begotten by them. Hence, Luke in his Gospel is understood to have taken as the father of Joseph, not him by whom Joseph was begotten, but him by whom Joseph was adopted; and it is the ancestors of this adoptive father who are recounted in an upward direction, until they reach David.

"But since it is necessary, as both Evangelists, namely Matthew and Luke, tell the truth, that one of them should show the origin of that father who begot Joseph, the other, the origin of him who adopted Joseph; which Evangelist do we think more probably shows the origin of the father who adopted Joseph, than the Evangelist who would not say that Joseph was 'begotten' by that man whose son the Evangelist says he was? Matthew, by saying Abraham begot Isaac, Isaac begot Jacob, and so continuing with the word: begot; until at last he says: Jacob begot Joseph; shows well enough that he was tracing the natural genealogy to that father by whom Joseph was not adopted, but begotten.

"Although even if Luke had said that Joseph was begotten by Heli, it should not upset our interpretation so as to think anything else than that by by one Evangelist is mentioned the natural father, and by the other the one who adopted Joseph. And it is not absurd to say of the son whom a man has adopted, that he is begotten by him, not in the flesh, but by charity. For even we, to whom God gave the power to be made His sons, are not begotten of His nature and substance, as His only Son, but are only adopted in love".

In this connection we should also like to quote a great spiritual writer, the Rev. M. Meschler, S. J.:

"This genealogy is of the highest import to St. Joseph, to his position and office, to his greatness and title to veneration; it is, first and foremost, the accepted genealogy of our saint himself. By means of it he is proved to be the son of David and is placed in the closest relationship to the promised Messias and God-Man, if not as real father, nevertheless as legally recognized parent. Thus, too, as regards the family of David, is the prophecy fulfilled that from one of its roots the Messiah would come forth (Ps. 83: 30; 1 Macch. 2: 57); hence, also it is proved that the Savior is truly the Son of David, and that the whole glory of this family culminates in Him through Joseph in a very particular manner. For Matthew calls Joseph's father Jacob (1: 16); Luke, however, styles him Heli, a difference which can only be explained on the supposition that in view of the Law of the Levirate (where a man was bound to marry the widow of his brother who had died childless, and thus perpetuate the latter's family) Jacob was the natural father of Joseph, while Heli was his legal father".

Before leaving this subject we consider it most helpful to quote the explanations of two of the greatest lights and Doctors of the Church — St. Ambrose, Archbishop of Milan, and St. John of Damascene:

"We might wonder why the lineal descent of Joseph rather than Mary, should be given, since Mary conceived Christ by the Holy Ghost, and Joseph appears to be unconnected with our Lord's birth, were it not that Holy Scripture teaches us that it was the custom to trace the descent on the male side. The personality of the male is emphasized: his dignity is maintained, even in the senate and the high places of the commonwealth. How unseemly it would be if, omitting the lineage on the father's side, that of the mother had been sought out; it would have appeared to proclaim to all the people in the world that Christ had no father! One sees that in every place, family genealogy is traced in the male line. Do not be perplexed at the lineage of Joseph being given. As Christ was born in the flesh, He was bound to follow the custom of the flesh, and He Who came into the world had to be enrolled in the worldly manner, especially as Joseph's descent was the same as Mary's.

"But why St. Matthew should begin to reckon the descent of Christ from Abraham, while Luke traces it from Christ up to God, seems to require explanation. Luke considers that Christ's lineage should be traced to God, because God was Christ's true progenitor, either as His Father according to His real begetting, or as the author of the mystical gift according to His re-birth in the laver of baptism. Therefore Luke does not begin to reckon Christ's lineage at the commencement (of His Gospel), but sets it forth after His baptism, wishing to show Him as God, the Author of all things, by baptism. Luke asserted also that Christ came forth from God in the order of succession, weaving all things together to prove Him to be both by nature, by grace, and by the flesh, the Son of God. But what more evident proof of His divine descent than that, just before speaking of His generation, he gives the words of the Father Himself: 'This is My beloved Son, in Whom I am well pleased'." (St. Ambrose.)

"Matthew begins his work with the words: The book of the generation of Jesus Christ, the son of Abraham; but he does not stop here; in fact he continues his narrative down to the Spouse of the Virgin. Luke, on the other hand, after relating the manifestation of the Savior at His baptism, makes a digression in his account, and writes thus: And Jesus Himself was beginning about the age of thirty years; being, as it was supposed, the son of Joseph, who was of Heli, who was of Mathat; and so on, in an ascending line, going up even to Seth, who was of Adam, who was of God. Then after reckoning up Joseph's genealogy in this way, it is shown clearly at the same time how Mary, who was herself also the Virgin Mother of God, was herself of the same lineage as Joseph. For indeed the Mosaic law forbade the marriages between the different tribes, so that the hereditary rights of one tribe might not pass into another.

"Nor without reason was the birth of Christ by the power of the Holy Ghost kept secret from the people, and that Joseph took the place of a father; and on that account, as was truly fitting, he was counted the father of the Child. If this had not been so, it would have seemed that the Child had no father, because He had no recorded descent on His father's side. Wherefore it was of the utmost importance that the Evangelists should record Joseph's origin. Had they not done so, but had given the Child's pedigree on His Mother's side, they would have done what would have been not only unseemly, but also opposed to the usage of the divine Scripture. It was therefore fitting that they should give the pedigree of Joseph from David, and for the reason which we have already given, of the kinship between her and her husband. They thereby attest that the Virgin Mary was of the lineage of David.

"It is indeed clear to all that Joseph was endued with justice, and led a life in accordance with the law. Therefore, living by what the law prescribed, he certainly would not marry a wife sprung from any other but his own tribe. If, then, Joseph belonged to the tribe of Juda and came of the stock and family of David, is it not a matter of course that Mary should come from the same? Whence it happens that her husband's descent is recorded. For if, according to the Apostle's saying, the head of the woman is the man, does it not follow in consequence that when the descent of the head is registered, that of the body is included in that of the head? I think it is therefore clearly shown, that the Evangelists purposely chronicle Joseph's genealogy, so that it is, in consequence, understood that the Virgin was also sprung of the family of David, and that by a surpassing miracle from her was born Christ, before all ages Son of God." (St. John of Damascene.)

In spite of the few facts related in the pages of Holy Scripture we are able to form a quite definite picture of the glorious Patriarch St. Joseph. We see him as the humble, obedient, chaste and holy carpenter of the small village of Nazareth. He was, as the Scriptures declare, "a just man". We learn that of all men he was chosen to be the guardian and protector of the Mother destined to give birth to Mankind's Redeemer.

GOD'S PROMISE OF A SAVIOR

We recall the promise made by God to Adam and Eve after their disobedience and fall from grace. Another opportunity for salvation was to be granted to them and their progeny. "I will put enmities between thee and the woman, and thy seed and her seed: she shall crush thy head, and thou shalt lie in wait for her heel." (Gen. 3: 15.)

Two thousand years had passed since those words were spoken when God made preparation for the fulfillment of the coming of the Savior, in the call of Abraham. An upright man, Abram by name, was to hear the call of the Most High God:

"Go forth out of thy country, and from thy

kindred, and out of thy father's house, and come into the land which I shall show thee". (Gen. 12: 1.)

In obedience Abram carried out the command of the Lord. Leaving Haran, his home, Abram journeyed as far as the place called Sichem, where a second promise was made, in the words:

"To thy seed will I give this land". (Gen. 12: 7.)

And continuing his travel he reached the land of the Canaanites and dwelt by the vale of Mambre, which is in Hebron. Here he was to hear the voice of God saying:

"All the land which thou seest, I will give to thee, and to thy seed forever. And I will make thy seed as the dust of the earth: if any man be able to number the dust of the earth, he shall be able to number thy seed also. Arise and walk through the land in the length, and in the breadth thereof: for I will give it to thee". (Gen. 13: 15-17.)

A great worry continued with Abram, namely, that he was without child, until God assured him:

"Look up to heaven, and number the stars, if thou canst. And He said to him: So shall thy seed be. Abram believed God, and it was reputed to him unto justice". (Gen. 15: 5, 6.)

When Abram had reached the high age of ninety-nine years, still dwelling in Mambre, God appeared to him and said:

"Neither shall thy name be called any more

Abram. But thou shalt be called Abraham: because I have made thee a father of many nations.... Sarai, thy wife, thou shalt not call Sarai, but Sara. And I will bless her, and of her I will give thee a son, whom I will bless: ... Sara, thy wife, shall bear thee a son: and thou shalt call his name Isaac". (Gen. 17: 5, 15, 16, 19.)

Months passed and the Lord fulfilled what He had spoken:

"And she conceived and bore a son in her old age, at the time that God had foretold her. And Abraham called the name of his son whom Sara bore him, Isaac". (Gen. 21: 2, 3.)

Abraham had now a son. To try his faith and obedience God commanded him:

"Take thy only-begotten son Isaac, whom thou lovest, and go into the land of vision: and there thou shalt offer him for an holocaust upon one of the mountains which I will show thee". (Gen. 22: 2.)

This Abraham promptly prepared to do. God, however, was testing the great Patriarch, and after stopping the sacrifice of Isaac, through the message of an Angel, He declared:

"Because thou hast done this thing, and hast not spared thy only-begotten son for My sake: I will bless thee, and I will multiply thy seed as the stars of heaven, and as the sand that is by the seashore. Thy seed shall possess the gates of their enemies. **And in thy seed shall all the nations of the earth be blessed;** because thou hast obeyed My voice". (Gen. 22: 16-18.)

Isaac had two sons, Esau and Jacob, who were twins, but unlike in every respect. Esau was loved by his father, and Jacob by his mother, Rebecca. As the first-born, Esau was entitled to the paternal blessing, but by means of deception Jacob obtained his brother's place. Realizing the consequences of his fatal mistake in selling his birthright for a mess of pottage, Esau conceived an implacable hatred against Jacob and threatened to kill him. At the advice of his mother, Jacob set out for Haran to visit his maternal uncle. When night overtook him on his journey, Jacob lay down on the ground to sleep and he dreamed:

"And he saw a ladder standing up on the earth, and the top thereof touching Heaven; and the Angels of God ascending and descending by it".

On this occasion the promise regarding the Savior was renewed to Jacob, the son of Isaac:

"I am the Lord, the God of Abraham thy father, and the God of Isaac. The land wherein thou sleepest, I will give to thee and to thy seed. And thy seed shall be as the dust of the earth . . . and **in thee and thy seed all the tribes of the earth shall be blessed.**" (Gen. 28: 12-14.)

In time Jacob married Rachel. They lived in

the land of Canaan. Jacob was blessed with twelve sons, who became the fathers of the twelve tribes of Israel. Jacob's favorite son was Joseph, the second youngest, and the one who followed most closely in the law of the Lord. For this reason he was hated by his brethren and by them sold into slavery and carried into Egypt. He was cast into prison and while there interpreted the dreams of the butler and baker, and later that of King Pharao. This pleased the Pharao very much and he made Joseph governor of Egypt. In this position by his great wisdom and foresight he saved the people from starvation. Before Jacob died we are to hear a renewal of the promise which God had made to him. Addressing his son Juda, he prophesied:

"The sceptre shall not be taken away from Juda, nor a ruler from his thigh, till He come that is to be sent, and He shall be the expectation of nations". (Gen. 49: 10.)

THE MOTHER OF THE SAVIOR

It is clear from what has been said that the Savior of Mankind was to come forth from the family of Abraham, Isaac and Jacob. And as the years passed, among the Israelites, the descendants of those three Patriarchs, God raised up Prophets —

Prophets that foretold that the Messiah would be born of a Virgin, of the tribe of Juda, of the House of David. The time of His advent was clearly indicated, as also the place of His birth — Bethlehem. "They called Him Wonderful, Counsellor, God the Mighty, the Father of the world to come, the Prince of Peace." (Gen. 12: 3; 22: 18; 49: 10; 2 Sam. 7: 12, 13; Ps. 89: 30, 37, 38; Dan. 7: 13, 14; Is. 7: 14; 2: 19; Jer. 23: 5; Is. 9: 5.)

Ever mindful of these promises the Jews hoped and prayed that the Messiah promised by Almighty God would come soon. Centuries were to pass.

The Israelites, for love of God, had erected a temple in Jerusalem, where they might offer Him sacrifice and worship. The costliest materials were used in the construction of the Temple, and its interior was overlaid with gold and silver and precious stones.

Since man would embellish God's dwelling place in such a wonderful manner, it is not difficult to conceive, rather it is to be expected, that God would prepare even a grander abode for His Son, Whom He was to send to redeem man, — not a temple of wood or stone, but the chaste womb of an Immaculate Virgin, which God had chosen to be the tabernacle of the Eternal Word. We can understand that the divine glory required that the person called to so high a destiny should be perfect.

Her heart, therefore, must be the most beautiful masterpiece from the hands of the Creator. Her purity must be so perfect that no human language can describe it, and no created intelligence conceive its excellence. Holy Scripture had sung its praise under the most beautiful figures. It compared the Mother of the Messiah sometimes to the cedar of Libanus, the wood which is incorruptible and the verdure perpetual; and sometimes to the lily of the valley which conceals its shining whiteness from the too brilliant rays of the sun.

And so, when God's hour arrived to carry out His promises, the Chosen One was born — immaculate from the first moment of her conception — free from original sin — filled with grace — a child of God. There appeared on earth the daughter of the holy spouses, Joachim and Anne, **Mary** — The Immaculate Conception, and "man's solitary boast"!

Pope Pius IX, on December 8, 1854, declared in his definition of the mystery of the Immaculate Conception:

"It was becoming that the ever blessed Virgin should be clothed in a garment of perfect sanctity, that she should be exempt from every stain of original sin, that she should win the most complete victory over the old serpent. For she was to be a Mother in every respect worthy of her Divine Son. She was to be chosen by God to be the Mother of

His only-begotten Son, Whom He loved as He loved Himself, and Who according to His nature was to be, at one and the same time, the Son of God the Father, and the Son of the Blessed Virgin. She was to be the Mother chosen by the Second Person of the Blessed Trinity. She it was from whom the Holy Ghost, by divine acts of His will and operation, was to cause Him to be born, from Whom He Himself proceeds. It was becoming that He Who has in Heaven a Father, Whom the seraphim praise as the thrice-holy God, should have on earth a mother who was not for a moment deprived of grace, innocence, or glory".

ESPOUSALS OF MARY AND JOSEPH

The common practice in the days of Mary was for Jewish girls to marry quite young. Consequently, when she attained her fourteenth year, at which age consecrated virgins left the Temple for their future homes, the High Priest desired Mary to marry, particularly since she was now an orphan; but she reminded him of her vow of virginity. In his embarrassment, the High Priest consulted the Lord; after which he summoned all the young men of the family of David, promising Mary in marriage to the one "whose rod should bloom".

Perhaps the High Priest was thinking of the prophecy of Isaias (chap. 11: 1), in which is foretold the spiritual kingdom of the Messias: "And there shall come forth a rod out of the root of Jesse, and a flower shall rise up out of his root".

Now an ancient tradition tells us that the lot fell to the holy, just, humble Joseph, and that his rod did actually bloom.

The faithful may learn considerable about St. Joseph from the revelations of the Blessed Virgin to the Venerable Sister Mary of Jesus of Agreda, a mystic of the 17th century in Spain, whose writings have been marked with ecclesiastical approval. (On March 14, 1729, Pope Benedict XIII decreed as follows: "It is ordered that the cause of the said servant of God shall be continued without any re-examination of 'The Mystical City', and her works may be kept and read". The Venerable servant of God declared that it was revealed to her by Mary, the spouse of St. Joseph, that when he was summoned to appear among the descendants of the family of David, in order that one of them be selected as the spouse of Mary, he was at that time thirty-three years of age, was well-favored in person and of most pleasing aspect, of incomparable modesty and grave in demeanor, and, above all, most pure in act, in thought, and in disposition, having, indeed, from the age of twelve years made a vow of chastity. He was related in the third degree to the Blessed Virgin, and his life had been most pure and holy and irreproachable in the eyes both of God and men.

From the office and position to which St. Joseph was chosen by Heaven we readily conclude that he was a man of greatest virtue and profound holiness. No other mere man was to hold a higher office. He would be "the Watchful Defender of Christ" and "the Chaste Guardian of Mary", the Virgin of virgins. As regards the saints of the Old Law, St. Joseph definitely surpassed them all in holiness. In him the holiness of all his ancestors, who in the designs of God were to cooperate in the accomplishment of the Incarnation, reached its culmination and perfection. Like Abraham, Joseph was a man of faith and obedience; like Isaac, a man of prayer and vision; like Jacob, a man of patience and self-sacrifice; like Joseph of Egypt, a man of purity; like David, a man according to God's own heart.

The foregoing thoughts are admirably expressed by St. Bernard of Clairvaux, the great lover and songster of Mary and her chaste spouse:

"Who and what manner of man this blessed Joseph was, you may conjecture from the name by which, a dispensation being allowed, he deserved to be so honored as to be believed and to be called the father of God. You may conjecture it from his very name, which, being interpreted, means Increase. At the same time remember that great man, the former Patriarch, who was sold into Egypt; and know that Joseph not only inherited the latter's name, but attained to his chastity, and equalled his grace and innocence.

"If then, that Joseph, sold by fraternal envy and carried into Egypt, foreshadowed the selling of Christ; this Joseph, flying from the envy of Herod, carried Christ into Egypt. The former, keeping faith with his lord, would have no intercourse with the lady; the latter, recognizing his Lady, the mother of his Lord, to be a virgin, and being himself chaste, guarded her faithfully. To the former was given discernment in the mysteries of dreams; to the latter it was given to know and to share in the heavenly mysteries.

"The former laid up wheat, not for himself but for all the people; the latter received the living Bread from heaven to guard it, for himself and for the whole world. There is no doubt that that Joseph, to whom the mother of the Savior was espoused, was a good and faithful man. A faithful and prudent servant, I say, whom the Lord gave as a consolation to His Mother, as the guardian of His own Body, and finally as the only and most faithful helper upon earth in the great plan of His Incarnation."

Joseph betrothed himself to the Virgin Mary, and she became his spouse. She dwelt in the little town of Nazareth, which nestled among the mountains to the north of the plain of Esdraelon in Palestine. The lives of the betrothed couple were spent in complete separation from each other. Joseph labored as a carpenter and Mary busied herself with prayer and her household duties.

THE INCARNATION

The hour of redemption had arrived. The winter was now passed and spring was returning to gladden the earth. According to many Doctors of the Church, it was the year 4,000 of the creation of the world, when an Archangel, of the highest rank of God's messengers, was summoned before the Adorable Trinity and commissioned to announce to Mary God's design regarding the wonderful mystery of the Eternal Son's Incarnation. Promptly the Archangel Gabriel, the same who had been commissioned to reveal to Daniel the time of the death of Mankind's Redeemer, winged his flight from the throne of God to Mary's humble dwelling in Nazareth. He found her absorbed in prayer. Reverently the Archangel bows and salutes God's chosen one, saying: "Hail, full of grace, the Lord is with thee; blessed art thou among women". (Luke 1: 28.)

Mary, troubled at his saying, wondered what manner of salutation this could be. So the angel said to her: "Fear not, Mary, for thou hast found grace with God. Behold, thou shalt conceive in thy womb, and shalt bring forth a son; and thou shalt call His name Jesus. He shall be great, and shall be called the Son of the Most High; and the Lord God shall give unto Him the throne of David His father; and He shall reign in the House of Jacob forever. And of His Kingdom there shall be no end".

Then Mary, recalling her solemn vow of chastity made to God, inquired of the angel: "How shall this be done, because I know not man?"

The Angel replied: "The Holy Ghost shall come upon thee, and the power of the Most High shall overshadow thee. And therefore also the Holy which shall be born of thee shall be called the Son of God. And behold, thy cousin Elizabeth, she also hath conceived a son in her old age; and this is the sixth month with her that is called barren: because no word shall be impossible with God".

In all humility Mary gave the answer on which depended the salvation of men: "Behold the handmaid of the Lord; be it done to me according to thy word". (Luke 1: 29-38.)

Mary's Son, now conceived by the Holy Ghost, is the Son of God, true God and true man. He is the long-awaited Messiah, the Redeemer of Mankind. and He shall reign in the House of Jacob forever.

O supreme moment, when the Mystery of the Incarnation of the Son of God took place. The instant the Blessed Virgin consented to be the Mother of the Savior the Child began to live. At that moment the Second Person of the Most Adorable Trinity, the Eternal Word, the Son of the living God, descended from Heaven, being hypostatically united to that soul and body, or humanity. Thus was effected **one divine Person in two distinct natures,** dwelling in the tabernacle of the chaste womb of the Blessed Virgin Mary.

With rare beauty Pope St. Leo the Great explained the doctrine of the Incarnation of Jesus to the faithful of his day:

"A royal virgin of the race of David is chosen to be pregnant with the sacred progeny, and to conceive the Divine and human offspring first in mind, then in body: and lest in ignorance of the heavenly counsel she should tremble at so strange an utterance, she learned from converse with the Angel that what is to be wrought in her, is of the Holy Ghost, and she did not believe it loss of honor that she is soon to be the Mother of God. For why should she be in despair over the novelty of such conception, to whom the power of the Most High has been promised to effect it? Her implicit faith is confirmed also by the attestation of a foregoing miracle. Elizabeth receives unexpected fecundity, in order that there may be no doubt that He, Who had given conception to the barren, would give it even to a Virgin".

And the great Pontiff and Doctor of the Church continues:

"Jesus Christ, our Lord, enters these lower parts, coming down from the heavenly throne, and yet not quitting His Father's glory, begotten in a new order, by a new nativity. In a new order, because being invisible in His own nature, He becomes visible to ours; the incomprehensible willed to be comprehended; existing before all time, He began to exist in time. And by a new birth He was begotten: conceived by a Virgin, born of a Virgin, without the concupiscence of a paternal body, without injury to the maternal chastity: since such an origin was seemly for the future Savior of men, Who should at the same time possess in Himself the substance of human nature, and also be ignorant of the stain of human lust. The origin is unlike, but the nature is like: He is free, as we believe from the use and wont of mankind: but by the power of God was it brought about, that a Virgin conceived, a Virgin brought forth, and a Virgin she remained".

As stated, Mary and Joseph were betrothed, not yet married; they lived apart at the time of the

Angel Gabriel's visit. Betrothed they awaited the day of the marriage. It was to the Virgin's humble dwelling in Nazareth that the Angel Gabriel came to ask her consent to become the Mother of the Redeemer.

After the departure of the Archangel Gabriel from the humble home, Mary remained a long time in ecstasy. The Word of God, the Eternal Son, Who was with God in the beginning, through Whom all things were made, had become Man in order to set man free from eternal death. Let us, with the holy angels, bow before this adorable Mystery of the Incarnation, in which is our salvation.

In explanation of the event just described St. Jerome answers the questions which might be asked concerning the mystery.

"Why was He (Jesus) conceived of an espoused virgin, rather than of one that was free? Firstly, that by the genealogy of Joseph the lineage of Mary might be shown. Secondly, lest she should be stoned by the Jews as an adulteress. Thirdly, that she might have a comforter when fleeing into Egypt. The Martyr Ignatius even added a fourth reason why He should have been conceived of an espoused virgin: That His birth, he says, might be concealed from the devil, since he would suppose that He had been born, not of a virgin, but of a married woman.

"Before they came together, she was found

with child of the Holy Ghost. She was found by Joseph only, not by anyone else, as he with almost the privilege of a husband, knew all that concerned his future wife. But when it is said: Before they came together: it does not follow that they came together afterwards; the Scripture merely says that they had not done so.

"Whereupon Joseph, her husband, being a just man and not willing publicly to expose her, was minded to put her away privately. If anyone is joined to an adulteress, he becomes one body with her, and, according to the Law, not only those who commit such a sin but also those who have knowledge of it are held guilty; how then could Joseph be described as just, if he had concealed the sin of his wife? But this is evidence for Mary; for Joseph, knowing her chastity, yet wondering what had happened, kept silence about the mystery he did not understand".

After the conception of our Lord, Mary, greatly moved by the wondrous words of the Archangel regarding her cousin Elizabeth (Luke 1: 36), lost no time in starting for a visit to her at Ain Kariin, where she dwelt with her husband Zachary. This visit was to be the first manifestation of the Incarnation and an application of its graces. Upon arrival, Mary greeted Elizabeth. "And it came to pass, that when Elizabeth heard the salutation of Mary, the infant leaped in her womb. And Elizabeth was filled with the Holy Ghost, and she cried out with a loud voice, and said:

"Blessed art thou among women, and blessed is the fruit of thy womb.

And whence is this to me, that the mother of my Lord should come to me?

For behold as soon as the voice of thy salutation sounded in my ears, the infant in my womb leaped for joy.

And blessed art thou that hast believed, because those things shall be accomplished that were spoken to thee by the Lord".

And Mary said: "My soul doth magnify the Lord". (Luke 1: 41-46.)

As Holy Scripture informs us, Mary remained with her cousin Elizabeth for about three months, when she returned to "her own house" in Nazareth to resume the discharge of her simple household duties. A great trial awaited her. She was betrothed to the holy carpenter Joseph, who was destined to guard her and her Divine Son.

Several months had elapsed since the memorable day of the Archangel's visit, and the heavenly mystery could not be concealed any longer. Joseph, who had a right to the secret of his betrothed, was a prey to the most intense grief. He was "a just man," faithfully observing the Law. He understood the extraordinary holiness and piety and innocence of Mary. He loved her, we are sure, above all created beings, and would readily have sacrificed his life for her. The most agonizing thoughts passed through his mind, and his heart ached. He was greatly troubled when he discovered that Mary was to be a mother.

On the other hand, it is not difficult to imagine the worried condition of Mary's soul. She had received from Almighty God the plenitude of graces. She was expected to correspond and cooperate with these graces. Observing Joseph's uneasiness, it pained her deeply; yet she **must** keep God's secret despite the severe trial her soul was undergoing. Deep humility and complete trust in God convinced her that this Mystery of His would be revealed by Him at the proper time.

During all ages Eastern maidens carefully practiced chastity. Moral delinquency among them was severely punished. And according to Jewish law a culprit met death by stoning (Deut. 22: 29). Owing to this severe law, St. Joseph, a just man, was thoroughly justified in being concerned, not so much for Mary's honor, but for her life. In consequence, after much reflection and prayer he found no other solution, in charity and justice, but "to put her away privately", as he was "not willing publicly to expose her" (Matt. 1: 19). "But while he thought on these things, behold the angel of the Lord appeared to him in sleep, saying: 'Joseph, son of David, fear not to take unto thee Mary thy wife, for that which is conceived in her is of the Holy Ghost, and she shall bring forth a son, and thou shalt call his name Jesus, for He shall save His people from their sins'. Now all this was done that it might be fulfilled which the Lord spoke by the prophet, saying: **Behold a virgin shall be with child, and bring forth a son, and they shall call His name Emmanuel**, which being interpreted is, **God with us**." (Matt. 1: 20-25.)

St. John Chrysostom, one of the greatest orators of all time, puts these words into the mouth of the Angel who addresses Joseph: "Mary will bring forth a son and you shall call His name Jesus. For you must not think that because He is of the Holy Spirit that you are thereby excluded from cooperating in this work of salvation. For even though you contributed nothing to His generation and even though the Virgin remained inviolate, nevertheless I confer on you that which belongs to a father, that you bestow the name on this son. 'For **you** will call Him.' Even if He is not your son, you will take a father's care of Him. Therefore, by the very imposition of His name I appoint you in the Father's stead".

After the Angel's revelation Joseph, convinced of Mary's innocence and of the great dignity God had bestowed upon him of being the foster-father of the Word Incarnate and the guardian of Mary, "concluded the ritual contract with Mary".* St. Matthew (1: 24) states clearly that "Joseph rising up from sleep did as the Angel of the Lord had commanded him, and took unto him his wife". Full of gratitude, St. Joseph fell upon his knees and bent himself to the ground to thank and praise Almighty God for these great mercies and graces. The bitter trial had served to bind the hearts of Mary and Joseph even more closely. And this was precisely God's design: to make known to each of them the virtue and sanctity of the other, and to unite their hearts in profound esteem and love.

The union of Mary and Joseph was, according to the teaching of the Church and the holy Fathers, a true and genuine marriage. St. Joseph was of a truth the husband of Mary and the legal father of Jesus Christ. The nuptial contract was the last preparation for the visible entrance of the Redeemer into the world. Daily Mary and Joseph endeavored to become more worthy of the high mission en-

---

*cf. A. J. Maas, Catholic Encyclopedia, Vol. XV. p. 464H, 1912 ed. Exegetes differ widely on this question.

trusted to them, holily passing the peaceful months that preceded the birth of the Savior.

If only it were given to us to understand the Mystery of the Incarnation and the persons involved, as seen with the eyes of St. Bernardine of Siena, who was chosen to be the great apostle of devotion to the Holy Name of Jesus, and of love of Mary! He explains:

"Since the marriage between Mary and Joseph was a real marriage contracted by divine inspiration, and since marriage involves so close a union of souls that the bridegroom and the bride are said to be one person, which may be called, as it were, the perfection of unity; how can any discerning person think that the Holy Ghost would unite, in such a union the soul of such a Virgin to any soul that did not closely resemble her in the works of virtue? Therefore I believe that this man, St. Joseph, was adorned with the most pure virginity, the most profound humility, the most ardent love and charity towards God, the loftiest contemplation. And since the Virgin knew that he was given her by the Holy Ghost to be her spouse, and the faithful guardian of her virginity, and to share besides in affectionate love and indulgent care towards the most divine Offspring of God; therefore I believe that she loved St. Joseph sincerely with all the affection of her heart.

"Joseph had the most ardent love for Christ. Who, pray, would deny that Christ, whether as a child or a grown man, would most deeply inspire ineffable sentiments and joys of His own in one who held Him in his arms and conversed with Him; and this together with the exterior grace of the filial gaze, speech, and embrace of Christ? O how sweet were the kisses he received from Him! O how sweet to hear the Little One lisp the name of father, and how delightful to feel His gentle embrace! Think again, when the little Jesus was growing big, and was wearied with much walking on the journeys they made, how Joseph, full of compassion, made Him rest in his bosom: for he bore towards Him all the fullness of an adoptive love, as to a most dear Son given to him by the Holy Ghost in his Virgin bride.

"So the most prudent Mother, who knew his affection, says to her Son Jesus, when she found Him in the Temple: 'Son, why hast Thou done so to us? Behold, Thy father and I have sought Thee sorrowing'. In order to understand this, we must note that Christ contains in Himself two savors: sweetness and sorrow; and since the most holy Joseph was in a wonderful manner a partaker of these two savors, therefore the blessed Virgin calls him in a special sense the father of Christ. This is the only place where we read that she did call St. Joseph the father of Jesus: because the sorrow which he felt at the loss of Jesus showed the fatherly affection he bore Him. For if according to human laws, which are approved by God, a man can adopt as his son the child of another family, how much more truly ought the Son of God, given to this Joseph in his most holy Spouse in the wonderful mystery of a virginal marriage, to be called his son; and it is also to be believed that in him there was the savor of paternal love and sorrow towards the beloved Jesus.

"Joseph was therefore not to be denied the name of father of Christ, merely because he did not beget Him by coition; seeing that he would also have been called the father of any child, not the issue of his wife, whom he might have adopted from another family. Christ was indeed thought to be the son of Joseph in another sense, namely, in that of having been actually begotten by him according to the flesh; but this was thought by those from whom Mary's virginity was concealed: for Luke says: 'And Jesus Himself was beginning about the age of thirty years; being (as was supposed) the son of Joseph'. Luke however does not hesitate to give the name of parent not only to Mary but to both parents, where he says: 'And the Child grew, and waxed strong, full of wisdom: and the grace of

God was in Him'. 'And His parents went every year to Jerusalem, at the solemn day of the pasch.' "

In like praise of St. Joseph, St. Bernard of Clairvaux reminded his listeners:

"There is no doubt that this Joseph, to whom the Mother of the Savior was espoused, was a good and faithful man. A faithful and prudent servant, I say, whom the Lord appointed to be the consolation of His Mother, the tutor of His own person, and the one faithful coadjutor on earth of His great counsel.

"Add to this that he is said to have been of the House of David. Truly indeed of the House of David; this Joseph was a true son of a race of kings, noble in descent, more noble in mind. A true son of David, no degenerate descendant of his father David; truly, I say, a son of David, not so much according to the flesh as in faith, holiness and devotion, whom, like another David, the Lord found to be a man after His own Heart; to whom He safely entrusted the most holy and hidden secret of His Heart; to whom, like another David, He showed the uncertain and hidden things of His wisdom, and granted that he should not be ignorant of a mystery which was known to none of the princes of this world.... What many kings and prophets desired to see, and saw not, desired to hear, and heard not; he was allowed not merely to hear and see, but also to carry, lead, embrace, kiss, nourish and protect.

"We must believe that Mary too, like Joseph, was descended from the House of David; otherwise she would not have been espoused to a man of the House of David, if she had not herself been of the House of David. Both therefore were of the House of David; but in one the truth, which the Lord had sworn to David was fulfilled; and the other knew and bore witness to the fulfillment of the promise."

THE JOURNEY TO BETHLEHEM

God's Will is often manifested to man through human events. As the days passed and the time approached when the Savior of the world would be born, Mary's blessed hands prepared the swaddling bands in which she would clothe the Infant God-Man. Mary and Joseph knew from Holy Scripture that He was to be born in the City of David: "And thou, Bethlehem Ephrata, art a little one among the thousands of Juda: out of thee shall He come forth unto Me that is to be the ruler in Israel; and His going forth is from the beginning, from the days of eternity" (Micheas 5: 2), but they did not know in what manner the promise would be fulfilled.

Mary and Joseph remained peacefully in Nazareth, although they realized that the time was near for the advent of the Redeemer. Because of their strong faith and complete abandonment to the leading of God's Providence, they were certain He would bring about His Will in the manner He pleased. They left all in His Hands. This time it was not by the message of an angel that they were to learn God's Will, but by an edict of the Roman Emperor, Caesar Augustus, that "the whole world" subject to him "should be enrolled". (Luke 2: 1.) Everyone was to go to his own city to have his name inscribed in the public register. Whatever motive the Emperor may have had for issuing the decree, he was, unknown to himself, serving the secret designs of God.

Since Joseph was of the house and family of David, he was obliged by the decree to be enrolled in Bethlehem, which was David's city. Thus God, by His over-ruling Providence, will bring about the fulfillment of the prophecy of Micheas, made several hundred years previously.

The decree was issued but a few days before the time when Mary's delivery was expected. When Joseph heard the Imperial word proclaimed with sound of trumpet in Nazareth he willingly submitted to it. He must have been greatly concerned, however, not for himself, but because of his solicitude for Mary who would have to make this journey of about 85 miles in her present condition, and in the depth of winter. But there was no delay. Mary cheerfully acquiesced in the Will of God, and encouraged and consoled her spouse. It did not take long to prepare for the journey, as Mary had everything ready for her expected child. A small supply of provisions was placed by Joseph upon the ass which would carry the Holy Virgin and the Incarnate God Himself.

It was towards the end of December, in the year 748 after the foundation of Rome, that the holy pilgrims set forth on their journey, as Caesar's order demanded. Mary mounted the beast of burden, and St. Joseph, with staff in one hand, seized the bridle of the faithful animal with the other. Thus they set forth on their long and tedious journey over the hilly, dusty roads down the slope of the Galilean hills and then across the Plain of Esdralon. Each day's journey was more fatiguing than the previous one, and the wind grew colder and more penetrating. We may be sure that those days were also days of privation and discomfort of every kind.

Continuing southward they came to Nablus, where they were able to rest. After passing through Silo, Bethel and Rama, they could see Mount Scopus and the Mount of Olives, and they knew that Jerusalem was close by. Mary and Joseph journeyed along slowly and modestly, with their thoughts centered on the Great Mystery about to be verified.

On the evening of the fifth day they approached Bethlehem. Travelers of every rank and age from the remotest parts of Judea were hurrying to that city to secure desirable lodgings. Many strangers had arrived there during the past few days to be enrolled in that little place.

As darkness was closing in that first Christmas eve Mary and Joseph entered Bethlehem. They sought lodging among the relatives and friends of St. Joseph, but no one would or could receive them, for the city was overcrowded. In vain they went from door to door, but everywhere the available space had already been taken. Even the guesthouse was full. The Evangelist simply says, "There was no room for them in the inn". (Luke 2: 7.)

It is not difficult to conceive the deep grief of St. Joseph and to imagine the thoughts of the Blessed Mother when they heard the words of the innkeepers on that first Christmas eve: "No room!" However, by far sadder to her maternal Heart is today's obstinate sinner who, by his conduct, says: "No room here for the Christ Child".

Let us admire the sweet serenity and patience of Mary. Silently she committed herself without reserve to Divine Providence to direct St. Joseph. It was his soul that was filled with anguish surpassing description. Turning to his spouse he said: "I remember having seen, outside the walls, a grotto used by shepherds. Let us go there, and if we find it unoccupied take up our lodging in it, as it is impossible to procure harbor here".

Weary though they were, Joseph led the ass which bore the Redeemer of the world and His Virgin Mother, and they retraced their steps. Not far from the eastern end of the city they found the cave in the rocks — a public stable, where the shepherds of Bethlehem sheltered their flocks during a storm. What must have been the confusion and sorrow of St. Joseph at having nothing better to offer to his august spouse! Nevertheless, it was in this poor place that the holy pilgrims decided to pass the night, and they thanked God from the depths of their hearts for having guided them to the shelter.

THE BIRTH OF THE SAVIOR

The moon, now high in the heavens, cast its silvery light through a crevice in the rock, which enabled them to see an ox which had been left there by shepherds, alongside of which St. Joseph tied the faithful beast which had carried Mary thus far. Then Joseph kindled a fire, for the cold was penetrating, and he and Mary sat beside it, partaking of the frugal viands which they had carried with them. Knowing that the hour was drawing near for the nativity of the Savior, Mary became more and more absorbed in contemplation. Presently she begged her holy spouse to withdraw and rest. With a rude lantern, though it cast a feeble ray, he discovered a quantity of straw. This he placed upon the ground, and Mary, gathering her robe and veil around her, continued absorbed in prayer. St. Joseph placed himself at the entrance to the cave as guardian, and united himself with the prayer of his spouse.

Then, to use the words of the Church on the Sunday within the octave of Christmas, "while all things were in quiet silence and the night was in the midst of her course, Thy Almighty Word, O Lord, came from Heaven, from Thy royal throne".

The Divine Child came into the world beautiful and resplendent, without detriment to the holy virginity of Mary. The Blessed Mother adored her Son and her God. St. Joseph was recalled from his ecstasy to behold and adore the Savior, Whom he had known only by revelation. He beheld the Divine Child in the arms of His Mother, and falling upon his knees adored Him with profound humility, kissing the Infant's feet with respectful tenderness. Then he presented to Mary the swaddling clothes that she had prepared, and with deep love she wrapped the Child in the "swaddling clothes and laid Him in the manger" (Luke 2: 7), in which had been placed hay and straw. Both kneeling down adored the King of the world made Man. They worshipped Him Whom they could call their Son, the King of Heaven and earth.

O sweet Infant Jesus, my God and my King, permit me to unite myself with thy dear Mother and St. Joseph in adoring Thee, and in offering Thee my heart and my love.

On this blessed Christmas night St. Joseph entered on the exercise of his prerogative of "father" of Jesus. That paternity, as has been shown, was far superior to a mere legal, that is, adopted paternity. Jesus, although not his true son, was much more than his adopted son. An adopted son is one who, born of strangers, is received into a home and then formally or legally invested with the title of son. Not so Jesus. Jesus was born miraculously of the Virgin Mary, the true and legitimate virgin spouse of St. Joseph. And all this, not by legal fiction, but by divine ordinance.

It is impossible for one to imagine the holy joy of Mary when she pressed to her heart Him Whom she had borne in her womb — this Son, Who is her God; nor will one be able to describe the joy of St. Joseph, who shared in Mary's happiness.

My loving Savior, grant men the grace to partake of the blissful emotions of Mary and Joseph in order that they may also be glad in the birth of the Redeemer.

THE ADORATION OF THE SHEPHERDS

This holy night brought another incident that warmed the hearts of Mary and Joseph. Scarcely had they offered their homage to the Savior when they heard footsteps and the voices of men, asking for admittance into the cave. They were those of humble shepherds who were keeping the night-watches over their flock on the Judean hills. They were the first to be privileged to receive the news of the Savior's birth, for soon after His nativity they beheld an angel of the Lord who stood by them, "and the brightness of the Lord shone round about them, and they feared with a great fear. And the angel said to them: 'Fear not; for, behold, I bring you tidings of great joy, that shall be to all the people; for, this day, is born to you a Savior, Who is Christ the Lord, in the city of David. And this shall be a sign unto you. You shall find the Infant wrapped in swaddling clothes, and laid in a manger'.

"And suddenly there was with the angel a multitude of the heavenly army, praising God, and saying 'Glory to God in the highest; and on earth peace to men of good will'.

"And it came to pass, after the angels departed from them into heaven, the shepherds said to one another: 'Let us go over to Bethlehem, and let us see this word that is come to pass, which the Lord hath showed to us'.

"And they came with haste; and they found Mary and Joseph, and the Infant lying in the manger. And seeing, they understood of the word that had been spoken to them concerning this Child. And all that heard, wondered; and at those things that were told them by the shepherds. But Mary kept all these words, pondering them in her heart". (Luke 2: 9-19.)

The shepherds' visit was a source of intense happiness to St. Joseph, because it was a recognition and an honoring of the Divine Child and Its Mother, and that He was already beginning His mission of mercy. St. Joseph presented the shepherds to Mary and through her to Jesus. He instructed them concerning the mission of Jesus Christ, which was to save His people. In this way did St. Joseph complete the heavenly message which the shepherds had received from the angels. Finally, he taught those simple men not by words alone, but by deeds as well, showing them how they were to adore the new-born Babe.

The faith, love and reverence exhibited by the holy Patriarch and his saintly spouse to the Divine Child could not but make a deep impression upon the souls of those simple men; hence, they "returned, glorifying and praising God for all the things they had heard and seen". (Luke 2: 20.)

Jacob had prophesied: "The sceptre shall not be taken away from Juda, nor a ruler from his thigh, till He come that is to be sent: and He shall be the expectation of nations". (Gen. 49: 10.) This prophecy was now fulfilled, as Herod, a foreigner, was ruling over Judea in the name of the Romans.

THE CIRCUMCISION AND NAMING OF THE DIVINE CHILD

Eight days after the birth of the Child He was circumcised, according to the precept laid upon Abraham and his descendants. "His name was called Jesus, which was called by the angel, before He was conceived in the womb." (Luke 2: 21.)

The Eternal Son of God subjected Himself to the painful and humiliating rite of the Hebrew dispensation, which was enjoined on sinners. Miraculously conceived, by the overshadowing of the Holy Ghost, Jesus was not subject to the law of circumcision. But He desired to subject Himself thereto in order to prove that He was truly a descendant of Abraham. Moreover, He would give sanction to the Old Law, because it was a Divine Law, which He recognized and observed perfectly. He thus sheds His Blood for the first time, and offers Himself as a Victim to His Heavenly Father for men. On Calvary He will pour out His life's Blood for man's Redemption.

The holy name "Jesus" signifies "Savior". It was not given to Him by Mary or by Joseph, or even by the Archangel Gabriel. The Angel was merely the bearer of a message from God, when he pronounced to Mary that the Child to be born of her was to be called "Jesus", as also when he appeared to St. Joseph in his sleep, saying: "Fear not to take unto thee Mary thy wife, for that which is conceived in her is of the Holy Ghost, and she shall bring forth a Son, and thou shalt call His name **Jesus**. For He shall save His people from their sins". (Matt. 1: 20, 21.)

Jesus is the Son of the Eternal Father; to the Eternal Father, therefore, it belonged to impose the name; and yet He commissioned St. Joseph to exercise that right in His place. St. Bernard teaches that the Holy Name of Jesus is the one, real Name of the **Word Made Flesh**, adding: "This is His Name from eternity. By nature He is the Savior: this Name is inborn to Him, not given by a creature, human or Angelic".

What great joy must have filled St. Joseph's

soul as he pronounced this ineffable Name for the first time! No father ever experienced greater consolation than did the holy Patriarch in pronouncing the Name of his beloved Son, for as the foster-father of Jesus, his heart was filled with the strongest and sweetest sentiments of love for the Divine Child.

THE PRESENTATION OF JESUS

The Holy Family remained in a poor house in Bethlehem until the time prescribed by the Law (Lev. 12: 2-8) when the mother of a male child had to present herself, forty days after the birth, for legal purification. Also, according to Exodus 13: 2 and Numbers 18: 15, the first-born son was to be offered to God at this time. Even though Mary and her Child were exempt, they complied with the law. Forty days after the birth of Jesus, Mary, accompanied by her holy spouse St. Joseph, wended their way to the Temple in Jerusalem to present Jesus to the Lord. Instead of a lamb, Mary and Joseph offered a pair of turtle-doves or two young pigeons — the sacrifice of the poor.

The ways of God are inscrutable, as St. Paul informs us; and so whilst Jesus, the Eternal Word, desired to have the glory of His Divinity concealed beneath His human nature, certain manifestations in His birth and the incidents of His earliest life were to be permitted so that all men would be inexcusable whilst those of "good will" would recognize the promised and long-desired Messiah. As He lay in the poor crib of Bethlehem Heaven testified, for His Angels announced His Divinity, and men, humble and virtuous, came to adore. A star arose in the skies to lead pious strangers, kings among their people, to seek the new-born Holy One among the Jews, Who was to be adored and, prophetically, through their gifts of gold, frankincense and myrrh, proclaimed the God of Heaven and the Savior of mankind. So, also, when Mary and Joseph arrived at the Temple — for her purification and her Son's presentation — Heaven desired to manifest the divine origin of the Child. Holy Scripture relates that the "just and devout" Simeon was also in Jerusalem "waiting for the consolation of Israel; and the Holy Ghost was in him. And he had received an answer from the Holy Ghost, that he should not see death before he had seen the Christ of the Lord, and he came by the Spirit into the Temple". At the moment when His parents brought in the Child Jesus to do for Him according to the custom of the law, Simeon took the Child into his arms, blessed God, and said:

"Now Thou dost dismiss thy servant, O Lord, according to Thy word in peace; because my eyes have seen Thy salvation, which Thou hast prepared before the face of all peoples: a light to the revelation of the Gentiles, and the glory of Thy people Israel". (Luke 2: 25-32.)

Mary and Joseph were wondering at the things which were spoken concerning the Child, when Simeon blessed them also, and said to Mary:

"Behold this **Child** is set for the fall and for the resurrection of many in Israel, and for a sign which shall be contradicted. And thy own soul a sword shall pierce, that, out of many hearts, thoughts may be revealed". (Luke 2: 34, 35.)

Mary and Joseph rejoiced, realizing that here was another who shared their secret and had come to worship the Hidden Savior.

Then there was an aged widow Anna, daughter of Phanuel, also in the Temple, where she served God day and night by fastings and prayers. She, too, praised God and spoke of the Infant Savior to all who awaited the redemption of Israel. (Luke 2: 36-38.)

We, who have been privileged to share in the secrets of the King, we who recognize Him daily at the Consecration of the Mass, and believe in His Divine Presence in the tabernacle in our Catholic churches, do we speak of the Eucharistic Lord to those who "know Him not"? Christian charity demands this! Oh, that all might be numbered among the followers of Jesus and share in the graces He longs to bestow upon them! Like Simeon, we see by faith what those outside the Catholic Church do not see. Let us not cease loving and praising God for His wonderful mercy to us, and constantly strive to bring the wandering sheep into His One, True Church.

THE ADORATION OF THE MAGI

Jesus was visited and adored first by the poor shepherds, considered the lowly of this world by those who loved grandeur and looked for a Messiah Who would come in a kingly state.

After the shepherds there arrived three Wise Men from the kingdoms of the East. They had discovered a new star. Enlightened by the Holy Ghost they assembled their attendants and mounting their camels started on the long journey in search of the new-born Messiah, King of the Jews — the promised Messiah. For, they were aware of the prophecy of Balaam: "A star shall rise out of Jacob, and a sceptre shall spring up from Israel". (Num. 24: 17.) Consequently, they were certain that the Redeemer had been born. They understood that they would encounter difficulties and hardships; maybe, also, the ridicule of their friends. But the grace of God had stirred their hearts, and they courageously resisted all temptations that might frustrate their plans.

Following the star until it brought them to Jerusalem, these Wise Men inquired of those whom they met where the new King could be found. As no one was able to give them the information desired they finally approached King Herod, asking: "Where is He that is born King of the Jews? For we have seen His star in the East and have come to adore Him".

"Herod was troubled, and all Jerusalem with him." (Matt. 2: 2, 3.)

Unable to answer the question of the three Wise Men, the king immediately assembled the chief priests, the scribes and other learned men, and inquired of them where the Christ was to be born. They said: "In Bethlehem of Juda. For so it is written by the prophet".

Suspicious and fearful, Herod then called the three Magi and inquired more carefully about the mysterious star and the exact time of its appearance, as he presumed that its appearance might have some bearing on the birth of the "new king". Having secured all the information possible, he advised the Magi to continue their journey to Bethlehem, and hypocritically urged them to return and inform him in the event they found this King, this Messiah, so that he might go and adore Him too. (Matt. 2: 8.)

The cunning, cruel monarch had no intention of paying homage to the "newborn King"; his real aim was to find Him so that he might the more easily put Him to death.

When the Magi left Herod's palace the blessed star again became visible, and joy filled their hearts. They followed it and soon "found the Child with Mary His Mother". After adoring their God, their Savior and King, they presented Him with the gifts of gold, frankincense and myrrh which they had brought. And, as they were ready to return home, God sent His Angel to warn them in sleep of Herod's treacherous and murderous intention. The Scriptures add that "they went back another way into their country". By this means God protected the Magi and frustrated the subtle, evil designs of the wicked king. Would that man understood that God will have His way. "Man proposes, but God disposes." (Imitation of Christ, Bk I, Chap. 19: 2.)

THE FLIGHT INTO EGYPT

Infuriated because the Wise Men failed to return and give the information regarding the Child, Herod immediately resolved to murder Jesus. However, like the many Herods of today, the first Herod failed to realize that there is a Higher Authority than that of an earthly king. The All-Knowing, All-Wise God, reading the mind of Herod, dispatched an Angel to Joseph, to warn him in a dream: "Arise, and take the Child and His Mother, and fly into Egypt, and be there until I shall tell thee. For, it will come to pass that Herod will seek the Child to destroy Him". (Matt. 2: 13.)

Herod had instructed his soldiers to kill every male child of two years and under in Bethlehem and in all the borders thereof.

We see that to Joseph, the head of the Holy Family, was entrusted the charge of preserving the life of the Christ Child. To him, alone, would redound this privilege. While all men would contribute to the death of the Savior, only one, St. Joseph, was to save Him from death in His infancy. Yet, it will be understood that a sword of sorrow pierced the heart of St. Joseph. The journey of one hundred and eighty miles would entail untold sacrifice and hardship. Saintly, obedient Joseph "arose and took the Child and His Mother by night, and retired into Egpyt: and He was there until the death of Herod". (Matt. 2: 14.)

One thing that stands out in the life of St. Joseph is his simple, unquestioning prompt obedience. It was sufficient for him to know that God wanted something done. He never stopped to question. He acted immediately.

Scarcely had the Holy Family left the confines of Bethlehem when lamentations and shrieks of horror rent the air. In vain, however, did Herod attempt to frustrate God's design, thereby fulfilling that which was spoken by Jeremias the prophet:

"A voice in Rama was heard, lamentation and great mourning: Rachel bewailing her children, and would not be comforted, because they are not". (Matt. 2: 16-18.)

The Blessed Virgin and St. Joseph abandoned themselves completely into God's hands, as they set out over the hill country of Judea through the dense forests to Hebron, the burial place of Abraham, Isaac and Jacob. Not venturing to enter the city, the Holy Family stopped to rest in a country-shed on the summit of a hill about a mile north of Hebron. The spot has preserved to this day the memory of the visit of the Mother of God in bearing her name, and the Arabs have not changed it. This stop-over has been a place of pious pilgrimage to Catholics through the centuries.

Whilst Holy Scripture does not tell us by what road the Holy Family fled into Egypt, it is reasonable to suppose that St. Joseph chose a direct route to Gaza on the Mediterranean, which would have taken about ten hours' travel. After another dismal nine days' journey through the little Arabian desert they would arrive at the River Nile, which they were obliged to cross. There, in Egypt, the Child Jesus would be safe from the wicked King Herod.

A life of exile in this far-away, strange country was for St. Joseph and his precious charges one of poverty, toil and suffering. But unbounded faith in God enabled them to be resigned to His holy Will. May we learn from their example to submit with resignation to the decrees of Divine Providence!

When the Empress St. Helena, mother of Constantine the Great, built the Church of the Nativity over the grotto of Bethlehem, many of the relics of the Holy Innocents were collected by her and placed in that church. Later a subterranean chapel was constructed and consecrated to these first Christian Martyrs. A pilgrim descends from the chapel of St. Joseph five steps to enter the chapel of the Holy Innocents. It has been the present writer's privilege to have visited this holy place, as well as all the places where Jesus, Mary and Joseph lived and died.

According to tradition, it was at Heliopolis, which is near Cairo, that the Holy Family abode during their exile in Egypt. At that time, in this city was the famous Temple of the Sun, praised by ancient writers, in which no less than 365 deities are said to have been worshipped.

The flight of the Incarnate Word into Egypt, Ven. Mary of Jesus of Agreda observes, had other ends in view besides the escape from Herod's fury — mysterious ends which had been foreshadowed in ancient prophecy. Our Lord, so to say, made this flight the means of accomplishing these, and went into Egypt to work in that land the miracles of which Ezechiel (30: 13) and Osee (11: 1), and, still more expressly, Isaias, had spoken:

"Behold the Lord will ascend upon a swift cloud, and will enter into Egypt, and the idols of Egypt shall be moved at His presence, and the heart of Egypt shall melt in the midst thereof". (Is. 19:1.)

Now all this came to pass when the Infant Jesus, borne in the arms of His Immaculate Virgin Mother, symbolized by a light cloud, came into that land. Ven. Mary of Jesus of Agreda adds that, before settling at Heliopolis, the Holy Family was led by angelic guidance to visit various other places where the Lord would work wonders and pour blessings on a benighted people; for the whole land was given up to idolatry and superstition. The Blessed Virgin Mary was so sweet and gentle in all her words, that they had a heavenly efficacy in them. Her countenance was so divinely beautiful that many were attracted to listen to her as she spoke of the true God Who made all things, and the vanity and falsehood of idols.

In Matarieh, between Heliopolis and Memphis, there still stands in a large orange grove a sycamore tree of enormous girth. It is claimed that it was here under its branches that the Holy Family rested. This tree is greatly venerated in the East, the Mohammedans calling it the tree of Jesus and Mary. About 100 feet distant is the Fountain of the Virgin, which is attributed to miraculous origin; which God caused to spring forth to allay the thirst of the Holy Family in a country parched by the burning rays of the sun. According to tradition, Mary drew water here and washed the swaddling bands of the Infant Jesus. For this reason the sick and infirm come to drink at this spring, and it is said that frequently they recover their health. Nearby is a large stone upon which the Virgin Mother would spread the linen to dry. These various spots are reverenced by both Christians and Mohammedans.

After the opening of the Suez Canal when the Empress Eugenie of France visited Egypt she went to see the ancient sycamore tree. Upon expressing a desire to possess it, the Viceroy of Egypt granted the request by presenting the tree to France. In order to protect it the Empress enclosed the tree with a handsome wrought-iron fence. She appointed two guards to protect the same, and also to cultivate lilies and jessamine within the enclosure.

The duration of the sojourn of the Holy Family in Egypt is conjectural. Upon St. Joseph rested the burdens of exile. Since God had entrusted him with the temporal welfare of the Holy Family, he toiled as a poor laborer daily in the sweat of his brow to support Jesus and Mary. Frequently he had to hear reproaches of some of the people, and to experience the coldness and indifference of others. Man never changes.

Ven. Mary of Jesus of Agreda declares that the Holy Family remained in exile six years. Other spiritual persons claim that it was for a much shorter period. Whatever the length of time, we know from Holy Scripture that it was upon the death of Herod that "An Angel of the Lord appeared in sleep to Joseph in Egypt, saying: 'Arise and take the Child and His Mother, and go into the land of Israel: for they are dead that sought the life of the Child' ". (Matt. 2: 19, 20.)

This message was a source of intense joy to Mary and Joseph, as they would soon see again the land of their birth. But they were sad as they recalled how the cruelty and ambition of the godless Herod had brought desolation and mourning to so many Jewish homes.

Joseph being a prudent man, immediately began to make preparations for their return. It will be noticed, however, that the Angel did not inform him of the place in Israel where they should abide. Knowing that God would reveal His holy Will in their regard in due time he "arose and took the Child and His Mother, and came into the land of Israel". (Matt. 2: 21.) Their journey was long and fatiguing. They had to endure many hardships over rough roads, sleeping out under Heaven's starlit canopy, as they recrossed the deserts they had traversed on their flight from the wicked ruler.

St. Joseph's only comfort and consolation in the midst of the tribulations and sufferings he was obliged to undergo while providing for the safety and welfare of the Word Incarnate and His Mother, was prayer — union with God.

When he heard that Archelaus reigned in Judea in the place of Herod, his father, he was afraid to go thither. He prayed for guidance and the angel appeared to him for the fourth time to direct him. "Being warned in sleep", the Gospel tells us, "he retired into the quarters of Galilee ... and dwelt in a city called Nazareth: that it might be fulfilled which was said by the prophets: 'That He shall be called a Nazarene' ". (Matt. 2: 22, 23.)

Mary and Joseph resumed their daily occupations in the humble home of Nazareth in order to provide for the care of the Divine Child. The earliest years of the life of Jesus are passed over in silence in Sacred Scripture, except for the one verse of St. Luke, after the Presentation in the Temple: "the Child grew and waxed strong, full of wisdom; and the grace of God was in Him" (2: 40). None of the acquaintances of the Holy Family suspected that the Child Jesus was different from any other child. He gave no evidence of anything superhuman about Him, and Mary and Joseph did not reveal the secret which God had entrusted to them. Their home was one of silence and holiness. In "silence" only, man contemplates God. Mary "pondered" in the interior solitude of her soul all that Jesus said and did. St. Joseph was a silent man. The Holy Gospels record not a single word of his. However, his silence is eloquent, insofar as it enables us to have a more perfect picture of his Virgin Spouse and her Divine Child. The silence of spirit of Mary and Joseph resulted from their victorious surrender to God's holy Will and their living in sweet companionship with Him. In silence they adored their God, and listened to Him Whom they loved above all things.

In the depths of every human soul there is rooted a craving for God. Few there are silent enough to recognize His voice within; for the cares and pleasures of life cover as with a pall the heart's desire to be united with the Lord and Savior. Real happiness which might come to man is sacrificed in a vain search for it where it is not to be found.

FINDING OF JESUS IN THE TEMPLE

The Mosaic Law required all adult male Israelites, unless legitimately prevented, to appear before God three times a year: — for the celebration of the Feast of Passover, for the Feast of Pentecost, and for the Feast of Tabernacles. (Ex. 34: 23.) Holy Scripture makes particular mention of the fact that the parents of Jesus every year journeyed to Jerusalem for the Pasch (Luke 2: 42), in commemoration of the preservation of all the first-born among the Israelites on the night when the first-born of the Egyptians were destroyed.

While only the men were obliged to visit the Temple on the three solemn feasts mentioned, the women frequently accompanied them. The boys in Israel, on reaching their twelfth year, were by law declared to be "of age", and thereafter bound by the legal precepts. St. Luke, in his Gospel, narrates that when Jesus was twelve years of age, His Mother and St. Joseph took Him to the Temple in Jerusalem for the celebration of the Pasch.

The Feast of Passover lasted seven days, during which time the Holy Family, as all other religious families, attended the services. It is a matter of history that the daily life of Jewish families was preeminently religious. For, on the doorpost, at the entrance of every home, there was, and is, fastened a **mezuzah,** a piece of parchment bearing the Commandments of the Lord (Deut. 6: 4-9; 11: 13-21), rolled up and enclosed in a wooden, metal, or glass case, which should be reverently touched by all who enter or depart.

At eventide of the fourteenth day of Nisan, i.e., March or April, the Paschal lamb was eaten; on the fifteenth day, the sacrificial ceremonies were performed in the Temple, which all men were obliged to attend. That same day, in the evening, in the presence of the people, the first sheaves of barley were cut and brought to the Temple to be offered to the Lord. They were burnt the following day. After this offering of the first fruits, the harvest season opened.

At the conclusion of the Feast, the numerous pilgrims began to wend their way homeward. This is probably what Joseph and Mary did. Now it was customary that on the first day of the return trip the men walked by themselves, the women by themselves, whilst the children attached themselves either to their father or mother. With hundreds of people in a caravan, there was bound to be confusion. Mary and Joseph naturally returned in the caravan going to Galilee, Joseph associating with the men and Mary with the women, as was the custom. The Child Jesus instead of uniting with one of these groups remained in Jerusalem.

As the sun declined in the west and the first day of the return-journey neared its end the caravan stopped for refreshment and the necessary preparations for the night's encampment. Then it was discovered that the Holy Child was missing. Great indeed was the anxiety and sorrow of His parents when they became aware that their beloved Son was lost. They feared for His safety. They knew not whether He had fallen into the hands of evil men that infested the countryside, whether Archelaus might have heard of the Child and ordered His arrest, or whether He had fallen prey, perhaps, to wild animals. In agony Mary sought Him among their kinsfolk and acquaintances, but without success.

Who will imagine the distress and the grief of St. Joseph over the loss of the Child Jesus? For he must have felt that in some way he had failed in his office of guardian, reproaching himself for permitting this unfortunate occurrence. And yet he was in no way to blame, for his thought was that Jesus accompanied His Mother, while Mary believed that He was with His foster-father.

The bereaved parents finally decided that there was but one thing to do, and that was to go back over the way they had come and look for the Child. They inquired of all the pilgrims they met, but no one had seen Him. On the third day they reached

Jerusalem. Here, again, they inquired of all they encountered; they went from house to house, but no one was able to offer a message of hope. No one knew where Jesus was. Afflicted, Mary and Joseph directed their steps to the Temple, and it was there that they found Jesus "sitting in the midst of the doctors, hearing them, and asking them questions. ... And seeing Him, they wondered. And His Mother said to Him: 'Son, why hast Thou done so to us? behold Thy father and I have sought Thee sorrowing'.

"And He said to them: 'How is it that you sought Me? Did you not know that I must be about My Father's business?'

"And they understood not the word that He spoke unto them.

"And He went down with them, and came to Nazareth, and was subject to them. And His Mother kept all these words in her heart.

"And Jesus advanced in wisdom, and age, and grace with God and men." (Luke 2: 42-52.)

Like Mary and Joseph all men should seek Jesus until they find Him.

Notable deeds in the work-life of St. Joseph are not recorded. He was the head of the Holy Family; to his care and protection were entrusted the Virgin Mary and her Divine Son. St. Joseph provided the necessities for his family by the industry of his hands as a carpenter, sanctifying all by prayer and good intentions. He was not called by God to perform miracles or to convert nations. Yet, today, it is known that no one ever implores his assistance without being aided; and many and great miracles have been performed through his intercession.

Like Mary, St. Joseph was to experience sorrows. Spiritual writers list seven of these: the thought of being obliged to send Mary away; the inability to find a fitting shelter on Christmas night; witnessing the sufferings of the Babe of Bethlehem during the Circumcision; Simeon's prophecy of sorrow to Mary, his beloved spouse; the Flight into Egypt; fear of Archelaus on the return from Egypt, and the loss of the Child Jesus in Jerusalem.

It is reasonable to suppose that St. Joseph, well versed in Holy Scripture, had knowledge of the prophecies regarding the Passion of his foster-Son; that He was the promised Redeemer, Who would be rejected by His own people, condemned to death, and crucified. Pondering these events surely must have caused him profound sorrow.

Yet amidst sorrow there can be joy; joy in a realization that whatever happens — sin excepted — is the Will of our Heavenly Father.

Spiritual writers also enumerate seven joys in the life of St. Joseph, namely: the assurance given to him by the Angel that Mary was innocent and that she had conceived miraculously; the adoration of the shepherds; the conferring of the Name "Jesus"; the adoration of the Magi; the announcement of Simeon that the Child would be the "resurrection of many in Israel"; the message of the Angel bidding the Holy Family to return from Egypt; and the finding of Jesus in the Temple.

And we unite with all spiritual writers in believing that St. Joseph's companionship with the Lily of Israel and her Divine Child brought untold joy, which increased his love for them daily. Could greater happiness be conceived than that which Joseph experienced when he held the Divine Babe to his breast, felt the touch of the Hands that created the world, listened to the voice that thrilled the nine choirs of Angels? Later in life when Jesus had grown into boyhood and manhood, what happiness to have Him for his constant companion in his humble workshop!

The Holy Family at Nazareth has been declared the model for all Christian homes. Such is the teaching of Pope Leo XIII in the Apostolic Letter, (**Neminem Fugit**), "It escapes no one", of June 14, 1892:

"When God in His mercy determined to accomplish the work of man's renewal, now through long ages awaited, He so appointed and ordained this work, that its very earliest beginnings might exhibit to the world the august spectacle of a Family divinely constituted, in which all men might behold a perfect model of domestic life, and of all virtue and holiness. For such indeed was that Family at Nazareth, where dwelt in secret the Sun of Justice, until the time when He should shine out in full splendor in the sight of all nations. Christ, our God and Savior, lived with His Virgin Mother, and with Joseph, a most holy man, who held to Him the place of father. There can be no doubt that every virtue called forth by an ordinary home life, with its mutual services of charity, its holy intercourse, and its practices of piety, was displayed in the highest degree in that Holy Family, since it was destined to be a pattern of all others. For that very reason was it established by the merciful designs of Providence, that every Christian, in every walk of life and in every place, might easily, if he would but give heed to it, have before him a motive and a pattern for the practice of every virtue.

"Truly, to fathers of families, Joseph is a superlative model of paternal vigilance and care. In the most holy Virgin Mother of God, mothers may find an excellent example of love, modesty, submission of spirit, and perfect faith. Whilst in Jesus, Who was subject to His parents, the children of the family have a Divine Model of obedience whom they can admire, reverence, and imitate. Those who are of noble birth may learn, from this Family of royal blood, how to live simply in times of prosperity, and how to retain their dignity in times of distress. The rich may learn that virtue is to be more esteemed than wealth. Artisans, and all such as are bitterly annoyed by the narrow and slender means of their families, if they would but consider the sublime holiness of the members of this domestic fellowship, could not fail to find cause for rejoicing in their lot, rather than for being dissatisfied with it. In common with the Holy Family, they have to work and provide for the daily wants of life. Joseph had to engage in trade in order to live; even the Divine Hands labored at an artisan's calling. It is not to be wondered at that the wealthiest men, if truly wise, have been willing to cast away their riches and to embrace a life of poverty with Jesus, Mary, and Joseph.

"In view of these considerations we may say that veneration of the Holy Family, if early introduced in the Catholic home, will steadily gain in vigor.... Nothing in fact can be conceived more helpful or effective for Christian families than the example of the Holy Family, embracing as it does the perfection and fulfillment of all domestic virtues.

"When thus invoked, may Jesus, Mary and Joseph take their place in the family circle as its propitious patrons. May they foster charity, mould character, and encourage the practice of virtue through imitation of their example; and by sweetening the burdens of this life which everywhere encompass us, may they render them more easy for us to bear."

A passage from the Pastoral Letter of one of the many Bishops of Nottingham, England, written in 1887 during the Holy Season of Advent, revives many of the thoughts already expressed. He describes the intimate love which prevailed in the Holy Family, as also the humble obedience and deference to Mary and St. Joseph by Jesus, true God from eternity:

"In the Holy House of Nazareth the Child was the teacher of His parents, not taught by them. The Eternal Wisdom of God could learn nothing from any creature, even in His human nature. Divine light, and teaching, and grace poured forth from His every act and word into the souls of His father and mother. Yet, while He thus enlightened them — the two most perfect of His creatures — His every look and word were those of a docile and obedient child. He followed their directions and obeyed their commands, and also the commands of His Heavenly Father, sent, not to Him directly, but to them for Him. He sat at their feet, hearing them and asking them questions, as He did with the priests in the Temple, while they always hung upon His words, and pondered them in their hearts, and wondered at His wisdom and at His answers. How marvellous must have been that school of Heavenly Wisdom, in which Mary and Joseph were but pupils, where even the Virgin of Good Counsel, the Seat of Wisdom herself, and her dear spouse Joseph, the just man, the Son of David, did not always comprehend the Word that was said, but had to ponder divine mysteries in their hearts, waiting for further illuminations of the Holy Spirit! What perfect and consummate wisdom was there breathed forth! What inconceivable perfection and holiness of life was there displayed! The angels who looked on in adoring admiration might have paraphrased the words of the prayer taught to the Apostles, and have besought God that His Will might be done by them in Heaven, as it was done by Jesus upon earth. For thirty years was Jesus subject to His parents, and for thirty years did that Paradise of Delights, the Holy House of Nazareth, continue to offer to us a model of every Christian virtue, a type and pattern of what our homes should be, or which, at least according to their measure, every home should imitate.

"Dear children in Christ", the Bishop continued, "visit in spirit that Holy House. Consider its poverty, and the rudeness and simplicity of its furniture. Behold also the exquisite cleanliness, order, and neatness which is manifested in every detail. Though poor, it is bright and cheerful, made so by the looks and words of loving hearts, and the labors of loving hands. The Eternal God, and the Queen of Heaven and her Spouse, chose not to have earthly magnificence around them. Had they possessed it, they, being perfect, would have sold what they had, and given to the poor. They chose the better part of voluntary poverty, working with their hands that even so they might have wherewith to give to those who were in need. They knew how many of the houses of their neighbors must be poor and destitute. Therefore they took their part in poverty and destitution, to show that the deepest poverty can be enriched and made happy by the love of God and man.

"How can we sufficiently admire the unremitting, uncomplaining, self-sacrificing toil of Joseph, who was honored by the Eternal Father with the office of governing and working for His Eternal Son and the Ever Blessed Virgin Mother! How shall we wonder at the sweet, gentle, assiduous labors of Mary, watching over the comfort of her husband and her Child, never forgetting nor omitting anything which might cheer or alleviate their earthly lot, and brightening their home with her beautiful and loving smiles! How shall we adore the gracious Child, advancing daily in wisdom, and age, and grace with God and man, manifesting ever more and more to His parents' wondering eyes the hidden perfections of His Godhead, and captivating their love by His reverent obedience, and sweet attentions, and gentle loving ways! What a school of love was there! Jesus, the ocean of created love and charity; Mary, full of grace and love as much as was possible to a pure creature; Joseph, the guardian-father of Jesus, the virgin-husband of Mary, the companion and disciple of both, and filled by God with that supreme love which such offices required. Every kind of created tenderness was there, ... There was the ineffable mutual love of husband for wife and of wife for husband, intensified as well as purified by the virginity of both. There was the love of father and the love of mother for their Child; for He was the Child of both, pre-ordained to be the recompense and bond of their virginal union. There was the love of the Child for His parents, intense and perfect, as must have been every kind of love in the Sacred Heart of God. ... There was the pattern of charity, piety, and mutual service and kindness, which should be imitated in every Catholic home. There was also a pattern of religious observance and of the worship of God. We read in the Holy Scriptures how perfectly our Lord and His parents observed the law of Moses, even when they might have justly claimed to be dispensed from it. We know He and His Blessed Mother and St. Joseph were ever engaged in unceasing love and contemplation of the Divinity. We can imagine, then, something of the solicitous attention, the reverence, and the devotion of the prayerful life of the Holy Family in their humble home. Prayer of the heart without ceasing, prayer in common many times a day, prayer undistracted, prayer made with adoring reverence in the visible presence of God, prayer enriched with the divine blessing of Him Who prayed.

"There also was the virtue of temperance in its perfection. In Jesus and Mary is found no evil passion to restrain, and in Joseph a Saint already made perfect in self-denial. Yet it lost nothing of its perfection or of the fullness of its practice. Obedience, self-sacrifice, humility, mortification of the appetites, meekness, chastity, modesty, sobriety — all concurred to the holiness and happiness of that home."

THE DEATH OF ST. JOSEPH

No doubt St. Joseph died during the hidden life of the Savior, since his name is not mentioned again in the Gospels either when Jesus left home to commence His public life, or at the marriage feast in

Cana, or in connection with any of the other episodes of Jesus' three years' ministry. Besides, if he was still living at the time of the crucifixion of Jesus, surely Jesus would not have confided His Mother to the care of St. John.

Moreover we learn from a book on the Life of the Blessed Virgin Mary, written by F. Amadeo de Caesare, M. C., Consultor of the Sacred Congregation of the Index, and which the author acknowledges as an abridgment of the "Mystical City of God" by the Venerable Mary of Jesus of Agreda, that "St. Joseph died at the age of sixty years". That "he had lived twenty-seven years with the Blessed Virgin, who, at the time of his decease, was forty-one years and six months old".

St. Joseph, the "just man", his mission accomplished, died the sweet and consoling death of the righteous!

* * *

St. Alphonsus Liguori, the founder of the Redemptorist Fathers, burned with love for the Blessed Sacrament and for Mary, the Mother of Jesus. What may not be known is that this same great saint inculcated into the hearts of his listeners a great confidence in the patronage of St. Joseph. In this connection, the late Cardinal Lepicier declared that St. Alphonsus, among other things, taught that the whole world acknowledges St. Joseph as the advocate of the dying, and this for three reasons: first, because being loved by Jesus not only as a friend but as a father, he possesses in Heaven a power of intercession greater than that of other saints; second, because he has special power over the demons who attack us on our death-bed, this privilege having been given him in recompense for the fact that he preserved the life of Jesus from the impious designs of Herod; and third, because of the assistance rendered him by Jesus and Mary at the hour of his death. In consequence St. Joseph has received the privilege of obtaining for his devout clients the inestimable grace of a holy and peaceful death in the sight of the Lord.

Jesus, Mary, Joseph, I give you my heart and my soul.

Jesus, Mary, Joseph, assist me in my last agony.

Jesus, Mary, Joseph, may I breathe forth my soul in peace with you.

THE GLORY OF ST. JOSEPH

Glorious and happy as was the death of St. Joseph, the gates of Heaven remained closed to him. Angels conducted his soul to Limbo, where a multitude of just and holy spirits of the Old Law were patiently awaiting the arrival of their Redeemer after the completion of His work on Golgotha's hill.

Faith teaches that the reward promised by God to those who serve Him faithfully is in proportion to the merits they acquired upon earth.

No one will imagine a grander, more sublime or meritorious position than that filled by St. Joseph. He cast protecting arms around Jesus, the God-Man, and his spouse, the Blessed Virgin Mary — the loveliest and holiest of creatures — when the life of the Child was endangered by the wicked King Herod and his soldiers. Thus he cooperated in the sublime work of our salvation. He endured sacrifices and privations of every kind. Many were the days of hard toil endured to provide for the needs of the Holy Family. As a carpenter St. Joseph glorified labor, since he was ever united with God and offered all in humble obedience to His Will.

Silently and humbly, patiently and lovingly he went about his daily tasks, never complaining; though his life could easily have been a monotonous and difficult one in the small workshop at Nazareth. As the foster-father of Jesus, it was his duty to teach the Child Jesus.

In the revelations of St. Bridget we have the Blessed Virgin saying: "My Son was so obedient that when Joseph said, 'Do this or that', immediately He did it".

Ven. Mary of Jesus of Agreda relates that when the Blessed Virgin understood that the final hour on earth of her faithful spouse was drawing near, she implored her Divine Son to assist him in the journey from life to eternity; and that she received more than she asked, namely a promise that He would not only assist St. Joseph, but "would raise him to a rank so exalted that he would be the admiration of all the celestial hierarchy".

In truth there must have been great rejoicing in Heaven when Jesus forty days after His Resurrection ascended triumphantly into Heaven accompanied by all the just who had lived from the beginning of creation and had been redeemed through the promise of Mankind's Savior. Foremost among these was His beloved foster-father St. Joseph, who, standing at the right hand of Jesus, was led by Him to occupy a place which, with the sole exception of that destined for Mary his holy spouse, was the highest in Heaven. He was enveloped in celestial joy at the vision of the Divine Essence, which no man can describe, as St. Paul wrote to the Corinthians (1 Cor. 2: 9): "Eye hath not seen, nor ear heard, neither hath it entered into the heart of man, what things God hath prepared for them that love Him".

In conclusion, Ven. Mary of Jesus of Agreda recounts extraordinary privileges granted by God to devout clients of St. Joseph:

"First, those who invoke him, shall obtain from God, by his intercession, the gift of chastity, and shall not be conquered by the temptations of the senses; second, these shall receive particular graces to deliver them from sin; third, they shall obtain a true devotion to the Blessed Virgin; fourth, they shall have a happy death, and in that all-decisive moment be defended against the assaults of Satan; fifth, they shall be delivered, if conducive to their salvation, from bodily sufferings, and shall find help in their afflictions; sixth, if married, they shall be blessed with off-spring; seventh, the demons shall have mortal dread of the invocation of the glorious name of St. Joseph".

St. Bernard sums up the life of St. Joseph with the words: "He was a faithful and prudent servant, I say, whom the Lord gave as a consolation to His Mother, as the guardian of His own Body, and finally as the only and most faithful helper upon earth in the great plan of His Incarnation".

St. Joseph, foster-father of our Lord Jesus Christ, and true spouse of Mary ever Virgin, pray for us!

PART II

Devotion to St. Joseph

When in Divine Providence the hour had arrived, an hour in which the Church found herself straitened by attacks of her enemies, God brought forth St. Joseph to shine as the Protector of His Church as he had been the Protector of its Founder, Jesus Christ.

Considering the remarkable sanctity of St. Joseph during his earthly life, and convinced of his unspeakable glory in Heaven, no Catholic will doubt his right to a deep devotion in his honor on the part of the faithful throughout the world. Moreover, since this holy Patriarch was the inseparable companion and faithful guardian of Mary on earth and the foster-father of Jesus, true Son of Mary, it is fitting and to be expected that he should partake of the honor and devotion shown by men to Jesus and Mary. Did not Jesus and Mary reverence him as the head of the Holy Family and submit perfectly to all his orders and dispositions? Their example will necessarily influence mankind.

At no time through the centuries was there a lack of holy souls who had a special devotion to the foster-father of Jesus, the Spouse of Mary. However, it was not the Will of God that exterior manifestation of this devotion to St. Joseph become universal before the hour "of God". Long years passed and the faithful were content to venerate St. Joseph implicitly in those mysteries in which he shared with Jesus and Mary; namely, the Incarnation, Circumcision, Adoration of the Magi, Presentation of Jesus in the Temple, and the Flight into Egypt.

Providence decreed that faith in the mystery of the Incarnation should first be implanted in Christian hearts before external devotion to St. Joseph be spread in the Church, thereby safeguarding the faithful from falling into one of the earlier heresies, the heresy that Jesus was the natural Son of St. Joseph. After the mystery of the virginal birth of our Savior was declared a dogma of faith, devotion to St. Joseph could become a more familiar practice with the faithful.

Gerson, a brilliant scholar and remarkable orator, Chancellor of the University of Paris, gave impetus to the devotion to St. Joseph in the beginning of the 15th century. Early in the 16th century, an Italian Capuchin monk, John of Fano, preached the Devotion of the Seven Sorrows of St. Joseph.

Since then Saints and Religious Orders in every century were especially devoted to St. Joseph. Churches were named in his honor. And after the

Council of Trent (1545-1563), Religious Orders vied with one another in placing themselves under the protection of St. Joseph, thus propagating devotion to the holy Patriarch.

Prophetically, a learned writer and preacher of the 16th century, Isidore of l'Isle, lifted his voice in praise:

"God raised up and glorified St. Joseph for the honor of His own Name, establishing him as head and patron of the Church Militant. **His glory is far from being at its height.** As, before the Last Judgment, all nations must know the name of, and venerate and adore, the only true God, so also must all admire the long-hidden, yet inestimable gifts whereof St. Joseph was the recipient. Yes, all gifts shall be granted unto him.... In that favored time, the Lord will give a more subtle intelligence to the minds and hearts of His elect; they shall scrutinize the heart of St. Joseph, to admire therein the loving marvels of grace, and they shall find an admirable treasure, such as the Patriarchs of the Old Law never either discovered or suspected. That magnificent outpouring of light and glory shall be the special work of the Holy Angels. Thus shall he who is first amongst the Saints of Heaven take, on earth, that first rank which is his due!"

A century later, Father Jacquinot, of the Society of Jesus, in like manner declared:

"Towards the end of the world God will tear asunder the veil which conceals from us the marvels of the shrine of Joseph's holy heart; the Holy Spirit will act on the hearts of the faithful, moving them to exalt the glory of that exalted personage; religious houses shall be consecrated and temples built in his honor, and people will recognize as a special protector that Saint who protected Jesus Christ; the Sovereign Pontiffs themselves shall decree, by a holy inspiration from above, that this great Patriarch be solemnly honored throughout the whole spiritual domain of St. Peter".

We have seen these prophecies fulfilled. Devotion to St. Joseph has made rapid progress; it has assumed proportions hitherto unknown. Joseph and Mary are united, or shall it be said "reunited", on earth as they are in Heaven. Like Mary, he has his temples, his altars, his festivals. The month of March is set apart for devotion to him, as well as the Wednesday of each week of the year.

On December 8, 1870, Pope Pius IX placed the entire Catholic Church under the patronage of St. Joseph with the title of Patron of the Universal Church.

The most recent exaltation of St. Joseph came from the pen of Pope Pius XI. In concluding his Encyclical "On Atheistic Communism", **Divini Redemptoris,** he declared St. Joseph to be the model and patron of the struggle against atheistic communism:

"To hasten the advent of the 'peace of Christ in the kingdom of Christ' so ardently desired by all, we place the vast campaign of the Church against world Communism under the standard of St. Joseph, her mighty Protector. He belongs to the working-class, and he bore the burdens of poverty for himself and the Holy Family, whose tender and vigilant head he was. To him was entrusted the Divine Child when Herod loosed his assassins against Him. In a life of faithful performance of everyday duties, he left an example for all those who must gain their bread by toil of their hands. He won for himself the title of 'The Just', serving thus as a living model of that Christian justice which should reign in social life".

St. Joseph is now venerated in every part of the world.

ST. JOSEPH, PATRON OF CANADA

In the early part of the 16th century there lived in Paris a priest, Jean Olier, who was renowned for his lofty virtues and works of zeal and charity. He was blessed in having St. Vincent de Paul for a director, and also Father de Condreu, Superior of the

Oratory. He founded the Company of St. Sulpice, and was destined to establish in Canada the devotion to the Holy Family.

At the same time there lived in Anjou a gentleman named Jerome le Royer de la Dauversiere, who was collector of taxes at La Fleche. He was a man of great piety, of rare abnegation, and the father of six children. God revealed to him, so the story goes, that He desired to be particularly honored in the Island of Montreal by the veneration of the Holy Family, and that He chose him to make St. Joseph honored.

On several occasions God ordered him to establish in Montreal, which was at that time barren and uncultivated and known as Ville Marie, a hospital for the relief and instruction of the sick, and to inaugurate a congregation of Hospital Nuns who would be specially devoted to the honor of St. Joseph, to manage the institution. M. de la Dauversiere was greatly perplexed, as he did not understand how, in his position of layman, he would be able to undertake such a task in America, particularly the establishment of a new congregation of women devoted to the service of St. Joseph. Up to that time he did not know of the Island of Montreal by name; nor would his financial means justify the undertaking of such large and important works. Nevertheless, as the orders were so frequently renewed in an urgent manner, with instructions clear and precise concerning the situation of Montreal and Canada, the quality and character of the persons who were to assist in executing the design, his confessor, who for a long time had considered the project impracticable, finally decided that he ought to let M. de la Dauversiere go to Paris to see if Providence would present him with an opportunity of carrying out this extraordinary enterprise.

Soon after he arrived in the capital of France he went to Mass at the Church of Notre Dame, and received Holy Communion with his usual fervor. Whilst making his thanksgiving, alone, near the statue of the Blessed Virgin Mary, and profoundly recollected, he was ravished out of himself and saw distinctly the Holy Family — Jesus, Mary and Joseph. As he contemplated these august personages, he heard Our Lord say these words three times to the Most Holy Virgin: "Where can I find a faithful servant?", and saw that Our Lady, taking himself by the hand, presented him to her Divine Son, saying: "Behold, Lord, this faithful servant". That then Our Lord received him kindly, and said, "Thou shalt henceforth be My faithful servant. I will clothe thee with wisdom and with strength; thou shalt have thine Angel Guardian for a guide. Labor earnestly at My work; My grace is sufficient for thee, and it shall not be wanting to thee". Whereupon the Savior placed in his hand a ring engraved with the names of **Jesus, Mary, Joseph,** and told him to give a similar one to all the young girls who would consecrate themselves to the Holy Family in the congregation he was going to establish.

Later M. de la Dauversiere went to Meudon to present himself to the Keeper of the Crown Seals. In the gallery of the castle he met the Reverend Jean Olier. They were not acquainted, had never seen each other, yet they embraced with the warmest affection, as though their hearts were one, and they saluted each other by name. Father Olier congratulated M. de la Dauversiere on the cause of his journey, and placing in his hands a roll of one hundred pounds in gold (about $500.00), said: "Sir, I want to share in the work; I know your intention, and am going to recommend it to God". The following morning M. de la Dauversiere received Holy Communion at the Mass offered by Father Olier. After the thanksgiving they retired to the park of the castle, and made known to each other the plans they had formulated to promote the glory of God in the Island of Montreal. It was clearly ascertained that both had received the same lights, the same orders, and proposed to take the same means to insure success.

Father Olier formed a company of pious persons, known as the Company of Our Lady of Montreal, most of whom were wealthy. They had been inspired by God to contribute by their prayers or their donations to the success of the work. Some time after, Father Olier assembled these persons and introduced M. de la Dauversiere, who related with simplicity the communications and orders he had received from God concerning this project. How strange soever such an enterprise might appear, the words of M. de la Dauversiere found an echo in those hearts so well disposed. All were convinced of his mission, and generously contributed to the work, considering themselves happy in being chosen to aid in the execution of the cause so advantageous for the glory of God and the welfare of His Church.

But, first, the Island of Montreal would have to be acquired. It was the property of M. de Lauson, who had received it from the Canada Company. On easy terms, forgetting his first intention regarding the Island and sacrificing great personal interests, he disposed of his holding. And soon thereafter the royal authority ratified the action. The intervention of Divine Providence was clear and manifest.

The Associates now pledged themselves to found a colony, and to establish three communities: First, a seminary of ecclesiastics, ten or twelve in number, destined to be Priests, to labor for the conversion of the early inhabitants of the Island, and to establish a school for boys; second, a community of religious teachers to educate girls; and, third, a hospital for the care of the sick. By these means the Associates hoped, through the goodness of God, to see in a short time the growth of a church which would imitate the purity and charity of the early Church. They further hoped that in succeeding years they and their successors could spread over the adjoining country, and erect new homes which would contribute to public convenience and facilitate the conversion of the Indians.

These three communities pledged themselves to honor Jesus, Mary and Joseph, each partaking of the spirit of their august patrons. The formal intention of the Associates was to confide the direction of the future Hospital to the religious whom M. de la Dauversiere would establish in honor of St. Joseph; the management of the Seminary to Father Olier, who shortly thereafter founded a Company well known in France under the name of St. Sulpice; and, finally, the community of teachers would be placed in charge of that person whom Providence might have chosen. This was Sister Bourgeoys, specially destined to make the Blessed Virgin Mary honored in Montreal. She founded the Congregation of Our Lady of Montreal.

The hundred Associates, under the name of the

Company of New France, in taking possession of Canada, had in view the formation of a French colony in Canada. They rejoiced in the thought that they could consecrate themselves entirely to God, and being aware of the fact that the Recollet Fathers had placed themselves under the patronage of St. Joseph, sent a statue of this holy patron, which was placed over the altar of Our Lady of Recovery (Notre Dame de Recouvrance).

As the adoption of St. Joseph for the first patron of Canada had not been made with all the requisite conditions while the Calvinists were in power, it was resolved to renew it with all the solemnities required by ecclesiastical law. It was therefore decreed that the magistrates and people, in union with the clergy, should ratify it in the most solemn manner. Pope Urban VIII sanctioned their choice by granting a plenary indulgence on the Feast of St. Joseph. On the eve of the festival, in the year 1637, a banner was raised and cannon fired announcing the next day's solemnity. Never before in that country had there been seen such brilliant fireworks as were displayed that same night. All the inhabitants of New France who were in the vicinity of Quebec had gathered to share in this public rejoicing. In the presence of all these people, the Governor himself lit the fireworks, the sudden splendor of which amazed the savages, especially the Hurons.

The following day, the Feast of St. Joseph, the church was as crowded as on Easter Sunday, each one praising God for having given the glorious St. Joseph, the Guardian of His Divine Son, as patron to New France.

ST. JOSEPH AND HUMBLE BROTHER ANDRE

The most beautiful Basilica on the American continent, located on Mount Royal, Montreal, Canada, is in honor of St. Joseph. It came into being through the prayers and devotion to this great Saint by the humble, saintly Brother Andre.

It was on August 9, 1845, that there was born at Saint Gregoire d'Iberville, in the Province of Quebec, Canada, Alfred Bessette, the sixth son of Isaac and Clothilde Foisey Bessette, the parents of eleven children. While poor, they were a loyal and deeply religious French-Canadian family, living a simple life in a log house. When Alfred was nine years old Mr. Bessette died, leaving his wife penniless with nine little children to care for. Unable to provide for them, she was forced to scatter the children among relatives for upbringing.

Alfred, always frail and sickly, was sent to the home of his uncle, Monsieur Timothee Nadeau of

St. Cesaire de Rouville, with whom he lived until he was fifteen years old. Owing to his poor health and the poverty of his parents, Alfred had been unable to attend school long enough to grasp even the rudiments of learning. His uncle was obliged to toil hard on his farm to support his family, and, consequently, had no time to instruct the boy. He was too frail to lend a helping hand to assist with any of the duties on the farm.

Alfred had loved his mother dearly, and longed for the day when he could be of service to her. But when he was twelve years of age, God called her to her eternal reward. Alfred felt the loss keenly and grieved much. Often, long after the rest of the family had retired for the night, the orphan boy was still on his knees offering up hundreds of "Aves" for his mother.

Like many other Canadian boys who desired to better their living conditions, he obtained a job in a cotton mill near Plainfield, Conn., but on account of his poor health he was obliged to give it up. He immediately sought employment as a handy man on a farm, but, again, was not able to hold this or similar jobs for any length of time. At the age of twenty-three he was convinced that the United States did not hold much promise of a future for him. He therefore returned to Canada and resided with relatives at Sutton, Quebec. Frequently he visited his former pastor, and it was to him that Alfred revealed that from early youth, when he had been an altar boy and served at Mass, he had a great desire to enter the service of his Lord and Master. He told of his ardent devotion to St. Joseph, and how he longed to spread devotion to him — the head of the Holy Family.

The Priest marvelled at Alfred's faith, but withheld judgment, knowing that he was unable to read or write and that he had a weak constitution. Nevertheless, God arranged affairs so that in 1870, the very year that St. Joseph was declared Patron of the Universal Church, Alfred Bessette, then twenty-five years of age, entered the Novitiate of the Congregation of the Holy Cross at St. Laurent. This Congregation was pledged in a special way to spread devotion to St. Joseph.

The youthful novice, who had received the name Brother Andre, was assigned to many hard tasks. He washed dishes and waited on the table; he scrubbed floors and mended clothes. After the beginning of his second year when he had renewed his vows, he was given his first assignment, that of porter at the College of Notre Dame at the foot of Mt. Royal, Montreal, which position he fulfilled faithfully for forty years. He won the affection of everyone with whom he came in contact because of his polite, gentle manner. The boys' parents always stopped to chat with him and to ask that he keep a special watch over their children.

When Brother Andre was not occupied with his task as porter he assisted with the washing of dishes, or with the cleaning and patching of the garments of the faculty and students. As there was no regular barbar in the vicinity of the College at that time, he acted in that capacity also, charging only five cents for a hair cut. His clients included all the students.

Brother Andre's great devotion to St. Joseph was a matter of general knowledge about the school. He always sought the aid of his patron for students, and devotion to St. Joseph spread rapidly among them. It was not long before the boys' parents learned about Brother Andre's prayers and sacrifices, and they began to ask that he remember them in his prayers. Extraordinary favors were received, with the result that the number of visitors to the College increased to ask his advice and prayers. From 1909 until his death on January 6, 1937, Brother Andre devoted his days to the sick and a considerable part of his nights to prayer.

There were those who were opposed to spreading devotion to St. Joseph, and they endeavored to curb it. Brother Andre ignored the attacks, and continued to perform his daily tasks faithfully and to pray. Not only the Catholics, but also the Protestants and Jews of Montreal were familiar with what he had accomplished, and they contributed freely to a fund to erect a chapel where he would be able to talk with and console the afflicted at any time.

During an illness of Brother Andre, Father Lecavalier, his superior, was also a patient in the college infirmary. They saw much of each other, and the favorite subject of the Brother's conversation was St. Joseph. Father Lecavalier was deeply impressed by the simple, childlike devotion of Brother Andre, and listened sympathetically to his earnest pleas for permission to construct a chapel where the Protector of the Holy Family might be honored in a special way. He finally gave permission for the college carpenter to erect the chapel, and for Brother Andre to spend for it the $200.00 he had saved from his earnings as a barber for the boys in the college.

In 1904, a little oratory fifteen feet by eighteen feet was built on Mount Royal, and dedicated that same year in honor of St. Joseph. It was to this little chapel that the humble Brother led the sick who sought his prayers, and there were many cures. A narrow, winding path led up the hillside to the shrine, which was hidden from the sight of passersby by large boulders and thick shrubbery. It was in this secluded spot that the holy Brother Andre retired daily and sought the intercession of St. Joseph for those who came to him for aid and advice. The pilgrims became so numerous that it became necessary to enlarge the primitive chapel. It was from this humble beginning that the magnificent Oratory of St. Joseph, now one of the greatest places of pilgrimage in the world, arose.

In 1917 the crypt of the beautiful Shrine was blessed, and on August 31, 1924, the corner-stone of the great Basilica was laid. The crypt in itself is a real church, being two hundred by seventy-five feet, and having a capacity of two thousand people. Rising above the main altar of the crypt is a statue nine feet high of the foster-father of Jesus, in his majestic mantle of Carrara marble, looking down with kindness upon the miseries which are daily disclosed at his feet. And a monument of St. Joseph, holding the Divine Infant, stands at the entrance to the grounds beckoning the pilgrims, about two million of whom visit the Oratory of St. Joseph annually.

In a spirit of penance and prayer and without the least embarrassment, pilgrims ascend the ninety-six steps leading to the crypt, on their knees.

The heart of Brother Andre is encased in a golden reliquary, which is exhibited in the Basilica, while his body is entombed in the crypt.

Millions of dollars were spent on preparing the foundation of this wonderful Shrine, on laying out and caring for the grounds, and for the erection of the Basilica (the interior of which is not yet completed). All these expenses were met without any appeal to the public, but simply through the gifts of St. Joseph's generous benefactors.

ST. JOSEPH, A GUARDIAN ANGEL

Amongst the numerous monuments that strike the eye of the traveller visiting Montreal for the first time is the magnificent hospital, known as the Hotel Dieu, on the slope of Mount Royal, commanding a view of the whole city. It is in charge of the Hospital Nuns of St. Joseph, which name they took when their Institute was established and the hospital was founded in the center of the city near the ancient church of Notre Dame. There it was that, for over two centuries, the Daughters of St. Joseph devotedly carried on their work of charity. There, too, occurred the incident we are about to relate.

The records show that at the time when the Reverend Mother Cleron directed the house of the Hospital Nuns of St. Joseph, in Montreal, the Lord conducted to His Sanctuary, in a marvellous manner, a young American Protestant, Frances Allen. She was the daughter of Ethan Allen the patriot, soldier of the Revolutionary War, and pioneer of the State of Vermont, and an atheist. Her mother, Francoise Montresor, lost her heroic husband when Frances was very young, and later married Dr. Jabez Penniman. While not an atheist, he was sufficiently averse to religion to exclude every thought of it, as far as possible, from his stepdaughter's mind.

Endowed with a precocious and penetrating mind, Miss Allen applied herself to reading. But having access only to romances and works by Deists, she became an unbeliever, even before knowing religious truths. Nevertheless, the natural rectitude of her judgment made her suspect that the truth could not be found in such works, and she frequently had conferences with her mother in an effort to discern the true from the false. Having heard people speak of Catholics unfavorably, she wished to ascertain whether what was said of them was true. When she was twenty-three years of age, she asked permission of her parents to go to Montreal. She foresaw that her stepfather, who was tenderly attached to her, would not probably consent to her going, fearing that she might embrace the Catholic religion. Therefore she did not disclose, then, the real motive of her journey. Instead, she gave as a reason that she desired to learn the French language, and Dr. Penniman yielded to her entreaties.

Nevertheless, before her departure, her parents required her to be baptized by the Reverend Daniel Barber, a Presbyterian minister of Claremont, New Hampshire. She long resisted their will, but, finally, to please her mother, she complied with their wishes. Being an unbeliever, she laughed during the ceremony, for which Mr. Barber reprimanded her severely.

Upon her arrival in Montreal, Miss Allen presented herself at the boarding-school of the Sisters of the Congregation of Our Lady. They willingly received her, hoping that while learning the French language she would gain the still more precious knowledge of the true faith. It was soon observed that she had a fixed adherence to her own opinions. It was only on the most indisputable proof that she accepted the views of others, and she never concealed from her teachers her incredulity in matters of religion.

One day one of the Sisters asked Miss Allen if she would not take a vase of flowers which had been given to her, and place it on the altar where the Blessed Sacrament reposed. At the same time she suggested that she adore Jesus Christ in the tabernacle. The young lady went off laughing, resolved to do nothing of the kind. When she opened the chapel door and attempted to step into the sanctuary, she felt herself suddenly stopped without power to go farther. Surprised at an obstacle so extraordinary, and after making three futile attempts to enter, she fell on her knees and, in the sincerity of her heart, adored Jesus Christ. Convinced of the Real Presence, she immediately retired to the rear of the chapel and bursting into tears she said: "After such a miracle, I must give myself up to my Savior".

She did not mention to her teachers what had occurred, but requested to be instructed in the Catholic Faith. Shortly afterwards she consented to go to confession. After completing the course of instruction she made her solemn abjuration, and was baptized by Father Le Saulnier, at that time Vicar of Montreal, her former baptism having been invalid by reason of the want of consent on her part. When she made her First Communion, she felt within her an unmistakable vocation to the religious life.

When Mr. and Mrs. Penniman were informed of the conversion of their daughter they were very much displeased and came to Montreal and took her home. Frances had much to suffer, especially from her stepfather, who was bitterly opposed to the Catholic religion. During Lent she rigorously observed the fast and abstinence, and carried her austerities so far that she injured her health, naturally very delicate.

Her parents endeavored to obliterate the idea of becoming a religious by bestowing on her every worldly pleasure and social enjoyment, but as soon as the year, which she had consented to pass with them before taking any step in the matter, was at an end, she declared to her parents that she had made her final decision and would embrace the religious life. Her mother, who loved her tenderly, and desired only her daughter's happiness, at length gave her consent and accompanied her to Montreal the following spring.

As yet, Miss Allen had not decided upon any particular community; her only desire was to consecrate herself to God in the religious life. In an effort to ascertain what God wanted of her, she visited the churches of Ville-Marie, and also the Hotel Dieu. Scarcely had she cast her eyes on the picture of the Holy Family over the main altar, and fixed them on the face of St. Joseph, than she cried aloud to her mother:

"That is just his portrait. You see, my dear mother, St. Joseph wants me here. He it was who saved my life, by delivering me from the monster that was going to devour me".

She then reminded her mother of a memorable fact that had taken place when she was about twelve years old. As she was walking on the banks of a river and looking at the water, which was in violent motion, she saw coming up out of it a huge animal, which approached her. She was greatly frightened. What increased her terror was that it seemed as though she could not take her eyes off this monster, and could not make the slightest attempt to fly.

In this fearful ordeal, she thought she perceived near her a bald old man clad in a brown cloak with a staff in his hand, who took her by the arm and enabled her to move, saying: "Little girl, what dost thou here? Fly." This she did quickly, and when a little way off, she turned to look at the old man, but there was no one to be seen. As soon as Frances reached home her mother, seeing her so scared and bewildered, realized that something unusual had occurred to her. The child related, as well as she could, the cause of her fright and the assistance she had received from the unknown old man. Immediately her mother sent a servant in search of the old man, in order to express her gratitude. After a most diligent search, no trace of him was found, and no one ever knew what had become of him.

The remembrance of his features was so stamped on Frances' mind, that, thirteen years later, when she cast her eyes upon the picture in the Hotel Dieu, she was struck with the identity of that face and garb, and could not help expressing her surprise aloud. She felt more confirmed than ever in her wish to embrace the religious life, and was convinced that she was to become a Daughter of St. Joseph.

Several months later, Frances Allen entered the novitiate of the Daughters of St. Joseph, and made her religious profession in the year 1810. The convent chapel was thronged with the many American friends who came to witness the strange spectacle of Ethan Allen's daughter becoming a Catholic nun. Till her death, which took place in the eleventh year after she entered the religious life, she justified by her zeal, her regularity, and all other Christian virtues, the hopes which the community had conceived of her after such a remarkable vocation.

ST. JOSEPH'S HOME
(The Holy House of Loreto)

After the Holy Sepulchre and St. Peter's in Rome, there is no place in all Christendom more famous as a place of pilgrimage than that of the most holy House of Loreto — the holy house of Nazareth, where dwelt Jesus, Mary and Joseph. It was venerated by Christians even during the lifetime of the Apostles, and St. Helena built a church around it, which received the name of St. Mary's.

Under the rule of the Arabian caliphs, a multitude of French pilgrims went to adore Jesus and to honor Mary and Joseph in that poor and lowly dwelling, where they led, for such a long period of time, a laborious and hidden life. But when the Turkish Seljoucides had enslaved their former masters, the pilgrims from Europe who ventured into Syria to visit Jerusalem and Nazareth were so barbarously treated that it roused to fury the entire West, which threw itself on Asia. When Godfrey de Boullion had been proclaimed king of Jerusalem, Tancred was named governor of Galilee. He had a great devotion to the Blessed Virgin Mary, and proved it by the sumptuous offerings wherewith he enriched the church of Nazareth. After the expedition of St. Louis, that corner of the earth, regarded as the cradle of Christianity, was defended, foot by foot, by the Knights of the Temple. These valiant warriors shed tears of rage and grief at the sight of the holy places profaned by the Saracens. Sometimes, forgetting the distance that separates the creature from the Creator, they carried their rash zeal so far as to be vexed with Him Who guides the course of human affairs, and reproached the God of Armies with the victories of their enemies.

Galilee, whitened with the bones of Latin warriors, had become Mohammedan. God was not willing that the Holy House of Mary should remain exposed to the profanation of the Infidels; He had it transported by Angels to a little mountain called Tersato in Sclavonia or Dalmatia. The miracles which were wrought daily in that house, the judicial investigation which deputies from Galilee made in Nazareth in order to establish the fact of the removal of this Holy House to Dalmatia, as well as the universal belief of the people from all nations who came to venerate it, seemed to be incontestable proofs of the truth of the prodigy. Nevertheless, it pleased God to give another proof, whereby all Italy and Dalmatia would be witness. After three years and seven months, the Holy House was transported across the Adriatic Sea to the territory of Recineti, in the March of Ancona, in the midst of a forest belonging to a pious and noble widow named Lauretta. According to ancient tradition, upon the arrival of the Holy House, the great trees of the forest bowed down in token of respect, remaining thus until the winds, the axe, or age laid them on the ground.

The Dalmatians were so grieved over this new removal that they could scarcely survive it. In order to console themselves they built, on the site where the Holy House had stood, a church which they consecrated to the Mother of God, since in charge of the Franciscans. On its door was placed this inscription: **Hic est locus in quo fuit sacra do-**

mus Nazarena, quae nunc in Recineti partibus colitur. (The sacred house of Nazareth once was here, and is now in the locality of Recineti.) Many of the Dalmatians even went to Italy to make their abode near the Holy House, and established there the Company of **Corpus Christi**, so-called by the Sclavonians until the pontificate of Paul III.

The news of this unusual event soon spread throughout Christendom, and an innumerable multitude of pilgrims came from many countries of Europe to Recineti to honor the Holy House of **Loreto,** as it was called. To establish more fully the truth of this miracle, the inhabitants of the province sent sixteen of their most qualified people to Dalmatia, and afterwards to Nazareth, to make a new investigation. But God Himself vouchsafed to make it manifest beyond all doubt, by suddenly renewing, twice in succession, the prodigy of the removal in the very territory of Recineti. At the end of eight months, the forest of Loreto having become infested with brigands who stopped pilgrims, the Holy House was transported a thousand miles away, and placed on a little height belonging to two brothers of the Antici family. When these two brothers took up arms against each other to divide the offerings of the pilgrims, the Holy House was transported to a place further off, on the main road, where it remained. It was there that the town of Loreto was afterwards built.

The church of Loreto has been magnificently adorned by the Sovereign Pontiffs, who have often gone there themselves on pilgrimage. Three doors of chased bronze give entrance to the holy edifice, in the center of which stands the Holy House in its garb of white marble, and adorned with superb bas-relief. The miraculous statue of Mary is carved in cedar wood, covered with magnificent drapery, standing on an altar resplendent with precious stones. The niche it occupies is lined with plates of gold, while lamps of massive silver burn night and day before it. May they be the pledge of our lasting love for the Immaculate Mother of the Savior!

Pope Benedict XIV, of immortal memory, the Bollandists, as well as many Pontifical Bulls, establish as a fact worthy of faith, that the Sanctuary of Our Lady of Loreto, venerated by Catholics everywhere, is the sacred house in which the Word of God was conceived, and which sheltered Jesus, Mary and Joseph during the Hidden Life of the Savior of mankind.

PART III

In Praise of St. Joseph

Doctors and Saints of the Church herald St. Joseph's high dignity in mankind's salvation:

St. Augustine

"Today is, as it were, a second birthday of the Savior. For we know that He was born with the same signs and wonders, but now there is a greater mystery in His baptism. For God says: 'This is My beloved Son, in Whom I am well pleased'. This second birth is indeed more glorious than the first. For then, He was born in silence, and without witnesses; now, the Lord is baptized with a proclamation of His Divinity. Then, Joseph, who was thought to be His father, excused himself; now, His true Father, Who was not believed to be so, introduces Himself. Then, the Mother was enduring suspicion, because no father was acknowledged; now she that bore Him is honored, because the Divinity makes Him known as His Son.

"I say that the second birth was more glorious than the first. For now, the God of Majesty records Himself as His Father; then, the workman Joseph was so accounted. And although in both cases it was the Holy Ghost through Whom the Lord was born and baptized, yet the Father, Whose voice was heard from Heaven, is greater than the father who labored on earth. Therefore Joseph the carpenter on earth was thought to be the father of the Lord and Savior. But God, the true Father of our Lord Jesus Christ, is not excluded from this trade, for He too is a carpenter.

"For He is the artificer Who hath wrought the fabric of this world with not merely wonderful, but with ineffable power. Like a wise architect He hath erected the heavens on high, He hath laid the foundations of the earth, He hath constrained the sea within its beaches. He is the artificer Who, in due measure, lowers the pinnacles of pride and brings to the surface the bedrock of humility. He is the artificer Who lops off the unnecessary material in our behavior and preserves whatever is useful. He is the artificer Whose axe, as John the Baptist warns us, is laid to the root of our tree, which if it departs from the rule of just discretion, may be torn up by the roots and consigned to the flames; but that which is according to the measure of truth, may be trimmed in the heavenly workshop".

* * *

St. Francis de Sales

[In a sermon preached on the Feast of St. Joseph to the

Sisters of the Visitation at Annecy, France, on the Virtues of St. Joseph.] *

" 'The just shall flourish like the palm-tree'. (Ps. 91: 13.) Thus does Holy Church make us sing on every feast-day of her saintly Confessors; but as the palm-tree has a great variety of special properties beyond all other trees — of which, indeed, it is the prince and king, as much on account of its beauty as of the excellence of its fruit — so there are also many varieties of justice. Although all the just may be just and equal in justice, nevertheless there is a great disproportion between the individual acts of their justice. This is figured by the robe of the Patriarch Joseph, which descended to his feet, and was embroidered with a rich variety of flowers. (Gen. 37: 3; 41: 42.) Every just man has the **robe of justice**, which descends to his feet (Is. 61: 10); that is to say, all the faculties and powers of his soul are covered with justice, and its interior and exterior represent justice itself, being just in all their impulses and in all their actions, internal as well as external. Yet, nevertheless, we must admit that each robe is embroidered with different beautiful varieties of flowers, the diversity of which does not

---

*(*The Spiritual Conferences of St. Francis de Sales*, published by the Newman Press, Westminister, Maryland.)

make them less pleasing or less worthy of admiration and commendation. The great St. Paul, the first hermit, was just with a most perfect justice, and yet it is undoubted that he never exercised so much charity towards the poor as St. John, who was called the Almoner on that account; nor had he ever any opportunities of practising hospitality, and therefore he did not possess that virtue in so high a degree as did many other saints. He had all the virtues, but not all of them in an equally high degree. Some of the saints excelled in one virtue, some in another, and although all have saved their souls, they have done so in very different ways, there being as many different kinds of sanctity as there are saints.

"This being presupposed, I will introduce my subject by observing that the palm-tree, among a great number of peculiar properties, has three special ones, which also belong in a remarkable manner to the Saint whose Feast we are keeping; that Saint of whom Holy Church bids us say that he is like to the **palm-tree**. Oh, what a great saint is the glorious St. Joseph! He is not only a Patriarch, but the chief and leader of the Patriarchs; he is not simply a Confessor, but more than a Confessor, for in him are enshrined the worth of Bishops, the generosity of Martyrs, and of all the other saints. It is, therefore, with reason that he is compared to the palm, which is the king of trees, and which has the properties of virginity, humility, courage and constancy, in all which virtues the glorious St. Joseph excelled so greatly. If we may venture to make comparisons, many would maintain that he surpasses all the other saints in these three virtues.

"Among palms, there are male and female trees. The male palm-tree does not bear fruit, and yet it is not unfruitful, for the female palm would bear no fruit without it, or without its aspect. So that if the female palm is not planted near the male palm-tree, and is not in sight of it, it remains unfruitful, and bears no dates, which are its fruit; but if, on the contrary, it is near the palm-tree and in sight of it, it bears a quantity of fruit, but quite purely and virginally. The palm-tree does not contribute any of its substance to this production; yet no one can say that it has not a great share in the fruit of the female palm, which without it would not bear any, but would remain barren and unfruitful.

"God having destined* from all eternity, in His divine Providence, that **a Virgin should conceive a Son** (Is. 7: 14), Who should be both God and man, willed nevertheless that this Virgin should be married. 'But, O God!' exclaim the holy Doctors, 'for

---
*determined

what reason didst Thou ordain two things so different, to be a virgin and bride at the same time?' Most of the Fathers say that this was in order to prevent Our Lady from being calumniated by the Jews. For they would assuredly not have exempted the Virgin Mother from opprobrium, and would have dared to constitute themselves judges of her purity. Therefore, in order to shield and protect this purity and virginity, it was necessary that Divine Providence should commit her to the charge and guardianship of a man absolutely pure, and that this Virgin should conceive and bring forth this sweet **fruit** (Cant. 2: 3) of life, Our Lord, under the shadow of holy marriage. St. Joseph, then, was like a palm-tree which, though bearing no fruit, is yet not unfruitful, but has a great share in the fruit of the female palm. Not that St. Joseph contributed anything towards that holy and glorious fruit, except indeed the shadow of marriage, which prevented Our Lady and glorious Mistress from being exposed to those calumnies and censures which the signs of her approaching Motherhood would have brought upon her. And although he contributed nothing of his own, yet he had a great part in this most holy fruit of his sacred Spouse. She belonged to him, and was planted close to him, like a glorious palm by the side of its beloved palm-tree, and, according to the decree of Divine Providence, could not produce fruit, and must not do so except under his shadow and in his sight; I mean, under the shadow of the holy marriage which they had contracted together, which was unlike the ordinary marriages of this world whether in respect of the communication of outward goods, or the union and conjunction of inward goods.

"Oh, divine union between Our Lady and the glorious St. Joseph! By means of this union, that Good of eternal goods, Our Lord Himself, belonged to St. Joseph as well as to Our Lady. This is not true as regards the nature which He took in the womb of our glorious Mistress, and which had been formed by the Holy Ghost of the most pure blood of Our Lady; but is so as regards grace, which made him participate in all the possessions of his beloved Spouse, and which increased so marvellously his growth in perfection; and this through his continual communication with Our Lady. For although it is true that she possessed every virtue in a higher degree than is attainable by any other pure creature, yet it is quite certain that the glorious St. Joseph was the being who approached most nearly to that perfection. And just as we see that a mirror placed opposite to the rays of the sun receives those rays perfectly, and another mirror placed opposite to the first, though it only takes or receives the sun's rays by reflection, yet reflects them so absolutely that you can scarcely judge which receives them directly from the sun and which only by reflection, so it was in the case of Our Lady. She was like a most pure mirror, receiving on a spotless surface the rays of the **Sun of Justice**, which poured into her soul all virtues in their perfection. All these virtues and perfections were then absolutely reflected in St. Joseph, so that it almost seemed as if he were as perfect, and possessed all virtues in as high a degree, as the glorious Virgin our Mistress.

"But, to continue our subject, in what degree, think you, did St. Joseph possess that virtue which makes us like to the Angels, the virtue of virginity? If the Blessed Virgin was not only a virgin all-pure and all-spotless, but even virginity itself (as Holy Church sings in the responses for the Lessons of Matins, 'Holy and immaculate Virginity', etc.), how great and supereminent in this virtue must not he have been who was appointed by the Eternal Father to be the guardian, or, to speak more truly, the companion of her virginity (for she needed no guard other than herself) — how great, I repeat, must not he have been in this respect? They had both vowed to keep their virginity all through their life, and this is why God willed them to be united by the bond of a holy marriage, not to make them gainsay or repent their vow, but to confirm them in it, and enable them to strengthen each other to persevere in their holy purpose. This is why they renewed their vow to live together in virginity all the rest of their life.

"The Spouse, in the Canticle of Canticles, (8: 8, 9), makes use of most admirable expressions to describe the modesty, chastity, and innocent candor of His divine love for His most dear Bride. He speaks thus: **Our sister is little, and hath no breasts. What shall we do to our sister in the day when she is to be spoken to? If she be a wall, let us build upon it bulwarks of silver: if she be a door, let us join it together with boards of cedar,** or with some other incorruptible wood. So speaks the divine Bridegroom of the purity of the Blessed Virgin, of the Church, or of the devout soul, but these words are chiefly addressed to the Blessed Virgin, who was pre-eminently this divine Sulamite. **Our sister is little and hath no breasts** — that is to say, thinks not of marriage, is not grown up to that estate. **What shall we do to her in the day when she is to be spoken to?** What does that mean? **In the day when she is to be spoken to?** Does not the Heavenly Bridegroom speak to her whenever He pleases? Yes, but by this expression is meant when marriage is spoken of to a maiden, and words spoken on this subject are of great importance, since it is a question of the choice and adoption of a vocation and state of life which is for all time. . . .

"The most glorious Virgin was a tower (Cant. 4: 4; 7: 4) and a high-walled enclosure into which the enemy could never enter. Neither could any desires find a place save the desire of living in perfect purity and virginity. **What shall we do to her?** for she ought to be married, He Who gave her this purpose to live a virgin, having thus ordained. If she be a tower **or a wall, let us set upon it bulwarks of silver,** which instead of breaking down the tower, will strengthen it the more. Well, what was the glorious St. Joseph but a strong bulwark built up upon Our Lady, since she, being his spouse, was subject to him and under his care? And he, so far from making use of this supremacy over Our Lady to break her vow of virginity, carried out the divine purpose which made him a sharer in that vow, while, by means also of their holy union, and under the veil and shelter of holy marriage, the purity of Our Lady could persevere all the more admirably in its integrity. **If the Blessed Virgin be a door**, says the Eternal Father, we will not that that door should be opened, for it is the Eastern Door, through which none may enter nor go forth. (Ezech. 44: 1, 2.) This closed door must be lined and strengthened with incorruptible wood — that is to say, we must give her a companion in her purity, the great St. Joseph, who must on that account surpass all the saints, nay even the Angels and the Cherubim, in that most admirable virtue of virginity, a virtue which makes him resemble the palm-tree, as we have already said.

"Let us pass on to the sacred peculiarity and virtue which I have observed in the palm-tree. There is, I consider, a most exact resemblance and conformity between St. Joseph and the palm in the great virtue of holy humility. For although the palm is the prince of trees, it is nevertheless the humblest, and the proof of this is that it hides its flowers in the springtime, when all other trees are displaying theirs, and does not put them forth till the summer heat is at its height. The palm keeps its blossoms shut up in little bags in the form of a sheath; and this very well represents the difference between souls aiming at perfection and others who are not — the difference between the just and those who live according to the ways of the world. For worldly and earthly-minded men, who are swayed by human laws, directly any good thought occurs to them, or any virtue stirs and animates them, become restlessly eager to display it and publish it abroad to all whom they meet. In doing this they run the same risk as trees which in the springtime are hasty in putting forth their blossoms — such as the almond-tree — for if by chance a frost surprises them, the blossoms perish and bear no fruit.

"Those worldly men who so lightly and hastily,

and in a spirit of pride and ambition, put forth all their blossoms in the springtime of this mortal life, always run the risk of being struck by a frost which destroys the fruit of their actions. On the contrary, the just always keep their blossoms closely shut up in the sheath of holy humility, and do not let them burst forth, if they can help it, till the time of great heat, when God, the divine **Sun of Justice,** will come into their hearts with all His mighty vivifying power, so that they may bring forth the sweet fruits of happiness and immortality. The palm does not show its blossoms until the burning heat of the sun has burst the sheaths in which they are enclosed, and almost immediately afterwards its fruit suddenly appears. So it is with the souls of the just; for they keep their blossoms — that is, their virtues — hidden under the veil of humility until death, when Our Lord suffers them to burst forth and be seen by all, being speedily followed by their fruits.

"Oh, how faithful in this was the great Saint of whom we are speaking! Words fail when we try to express the perfection of this fidelity; for consider in what poverty and abjection he lived throughout his whole life; and what great virtue and dignity he kept concealed beneath that same poverty and abjection! What a dignity to be the guardian of Our Lord, and not only that, but to be even His reputed father, to be the husband of His most holy Mother! Truly, I doubt not that the Angels, wondering and adoring, came thronging in countless multitudes to that poor workshop to admire the humility of him who guarded that dear and divine Child, and labored at his carpenter's trade to support the Son and the Mother who were committed to his care.

"There is no doubt, my dear Sisters, that St. Joseph was more valiant than David and wiser than Solomon; nevertheless, seeing him so humbly working in his carpenter's shop, who would have imagined (unless enlightened supernaturally) that he was endowed by God with such marvellous gifts, so closely and carefully did he keep them concealed! But what must not his wisdom have been, seeing that God committed to his charge His all-glorious Son and chose him to be His guardian! If earthly princes consider it a matter of so much importance to select carefully a tutor fit for their children, think you that the Eternal God would not, in His almighty power and wisdom, choose from out of His creation the most perfect man living to be the guardian of His divine and most glorious Son, the Prince of heaven and earth? There is, then, no doubt at all that St. Joseph was endowed with all gifts and graces required by the charge which the Eternal Father willed to commit to him, over all the domestic and temporal concerns of Our Lord, and the guidance of his family, which was composed of three persons only, representing to us the mystery of the Most Holy and Adorable Trinity. Not that there is any real comparison in this matter excepting as regards Our Lord, Who is one of the Persons of the Most Blessed Trinity, for the others were but creatures; yet still we may say that it was a trinity on earth representing in some sort the Most Holy Trinity. Mary, Jesus, and Joseph — Joseph, Jesus, and Mary — a trinity worthy indeed to be honored and greatly esteemed!

"You understand, then, how exalted was the dignity of St. Joseph and how full he was of all virtue. And yet you see how deeply he was abased and humbled, more than we can ever say or imagine. One instance alone is sufficient to prove this: he went into his own country and to his own town of Bethlehem, and, as far as we know, he alone was refused admittance into any of the inns, so that he was constrained to retire, and to conduct his most chaste Spouse into a stable among oxen and asses. (Luke 2: 4-7.) Oh, to what an extremity of abjection and humiliation was he not reduced! His humility also, as St. Bernard explains, was the cause of his wishing to quit Our Lady when he saw that she was with child; for St. Bernard says that he spoke thus to himself: 'Ah! what is this? I know that she is a virgin, for we have together made a vow to keep our virginity and purity intact — a vow which nothing would induce her to break; yet I see that she is with child. How can it be that maternity is found in virginity, and that virginity does not hinder maternity? O my God! must not this be that glorious Virgin of whom the Prophets declare that **she shall conceive** and be the Mother of the Messiah? (Is. 7: 14.) Oh, if this is so, God forbid that I should remain with her — I, who am so unworthy of such an honor! Better far that I should quit her secretly on account of my unworthiness, and that I should dwell no longer in her company'. What admirable humility! It was the same feeling which stirred St. Peter when he was in the boat with Our Lord and had seen His almighty power manifested in the great draught of fishes, following instantly upon their obeying His command to cast their nets into the sea; a feeling of overwhelming humility making him cry out: 'Depart from me, O Lord, for I am a sinful man', unworthy to be with Thee. 'I know', he seems to say, 'that if I throw myself into the sea I shall perish, but Thou Who art Almighty canst walk without danger upon the waters, therefore I entreat Thee to depart from me, rather than that I should depart from Thee.' But if St. Joseph was careful to keep his virtues safely concealed under the shelter of holy humility, he was especially so with regard to the precious pearl of his virginity. For this reason he consented to be married, in order that no one might be aware of it, and that under the veil of holy marriage he might lead a still more hidden life. So, too, all men and women who wish to live a life of perfect chastity and virginity, are taught that this is not enough, and avails little if they are not also humble, locking up this treasure of purity in the precious casket of humility. If they fail to do this, they will be like the foolish virgins who, for want of humility and merciful charity, were shut out from the marriage feast of the Bridegroom, and were thus constrained to be guests only at the marriage feast on earth, where the counsel given by the heavenly Bridegroom is not observed. He says (Luke 14: 8, 10) — thus inculcating the practice of humility — 'Going or **being invited** to the marriage feast, **take the lowest place**'. Thus we see how necessary humility is for the preservation of virginity, since, undoubtedly none will be admitted to the heavenly banquet — that marriage feast which God prepares for Virgins in the celestial kingdom — unless they take with them this virtue.

"We do not keep precious things, especially such as sweet-smelling ointments, uncovered and exposed to the air, for not only would their perfume waste itself and evaporate, but also flies would spoil them and make them lose their price and value. So, too, the souls of the just, fearing to lose the price and value of their good works, lock them up generally in a box, but not in a common one, rather in a box of alabaster, like precious ointment, such as that which St. Mary Magdalen poured upon the Sacred Head of our Divine Lord, when He restored her to a virginity, not indeed essential, but repaired. This is sometimes the most excellent kind, being acquired and re-established by penance, whereas that which is wholly unblemished is, or may be, accompanied by less humility. This alabaster box is, then, humility, in which we, imitating Our Lady and St. Joseph, ought to lock up our virtues and all that can make us esteemed by men, and be content to please God and remain hidden under the blessed veil of self-humiliation; we must wait, as we have said, until God Himself shall come to take us into the place of safety, which is Life Eternal, and shall Himself manifest our virtues for His own honor and glory.

"But what more perfect humility can be imagined than that of St. Joseph? I put aside that of Our Lady, for we have already said that St. Joseph received a great increase of all virtues by the reflection of those of the Blessed Virgin. He had a very great share in the divine treasure, Our Lord and Master, which he guarded in his house, and yet he behaved so meekly and humbly that it appeared as if he had no part in it. Yet no one can doubt that the Holy Child, being of St. Joseph's family, and the Son of his own Spouse, belonged to him more than to any other excepting Our Blessed Lady. If a dove (to render the comparison more suitable to the purity of the Saints of whom I am speaking) carried in her beak a date which she let fall into a garden, would you not say that the palm-tree which sprang up from the date belonged to the owner of the garden? Well, if that is so, who can doubt that the Holy Ghost, like a holy Dove, having let fall this divine date into the enclosed and shut-up garden of the Blessed Virgin, a **garden sealed** (Cant. 4: 12) and hedged in on all sides by the sacred vow of virginity and immaculate chastity, which belonged to St. Joseph as the bride to her husband — who can doubt, I repeat, that this divine palm-tree, which bears fruit of immortal nourishment, belongs most truly to St. Joseph, who yet, instead of becoming prouder on that account, becomes more humble?

"How good it is to see the reverence and respect of all our Saint's dealings and intercourse both with the Mother and the Son! If he had for a moment wished to quit the Mother, not then fully understanding the greatness of his dignity, with what admiration and profound self-abasement was he not afterwards overwhelmed when he saw himself so much honored by **Our Lord** and **Our Lady**, who actually obeyed his will and did only what he commanded! This, indeed, is a thing beyond comprehension, and we must therefore pass on to the third property we remark in the palm — namely, a marvellous union of courage, constancy, and strength — virtues which are pre-eminently found in our Saint.

"The palm has a strength, courage and even constancy far beyond all other trees, therefore it takes the highest rank among them. The palm shows its strength in this, that the more it is laden, the more it shoots up and the higher it grows; which is quite unlike all other trees, and indeed all other things, for the more heavily they are laden, the more they bow down to the earth. The palm, however, shows its strength and constancy, never bending down, whatever load is placed upon it. It is its instinct to shoot upwards, and nothing can prevent it from doing so. It shows its valor in its sword-shaped foliage, and seems, therefore, to have as many weapons of defense as it has leaves.

"Certainly St. Joseph is most justly said to resemble the palm, for he was always constant, persevering, strong, and valiant. There is a great difference between these four virtues. We call a man constant when he remains firm, and prepared to suffer the assaults of the enemy, without surprise or loss of courage during the combat. Perseverance, however, has chiefly to do with a certain weariness of mind which comes upon us when we have suffered a long time, and this weariness is as powerful an enemy as we can meet with. Now, perseverance enables a man so to disregard this enemy that he gains the victory over it by continual calmness and submission to the Will of God. Strength makes a man vigorously resist the attacks of his enemies. And valor is a virtue which makes us not only hold ourselves in readiness to fight or to offer resistance when the occasion presents itself, but also to attack the enemy at the moment when he least expects it.

"Now, our glorious St. Joseph was endowed with all these virtues, and practised them marvellously well. As regards his constancy, did he not display it wonderfully when, seeing Our Lady with child, and not knowing how that could be, his mind was tossed with distress, perplexity, and trouble? Yet, in spite of all, he never complained, he was never harsh or ungracious towards his holy Spouse, but remained just as gentle and respectful in his demeanor as he had ever been. But what valor and strength did he not display in the victory which he gained over the two greatest enemies of man, the devil and the world? And that by practice of a most perfect humility, as we have said, throughout the whole course of his life. The devil, who for want of humility, and because he would not accept it for his inseparable companion, was driven out of Heaven and cast down into Hell, is so great an enemy to the lowly virtue, that there is no artifice or invention he will not use to make men fall away from it — so much the more because it is a virtue which renders them infinitely pleasing to God. We may, therefore, well say: 'Valiant and strong is the man who, like St. Joseph, perseveres in humility; he will be conquerer at once of the devil and of the world, which is full of ambition, vanity and pride'.

"As regards perseverance, which overcomes that secret enemy of our souls, weariness and dejection under the continued assaults of humbling, painful circumstances — ill fortune, as we say — and the thousand accidents and misadventures of daily life, how greatly was the Saint tried in this way by God and man in his journey into Egypt! The Angel commanded him to set forth immediately and to take Our Lady and the Holy Child into that country. (Matt. 2: 13, 14.) Instantly, without a moment's delay, without even a word, he obeys. He does not ask: 'Where shall I go? What road shall I take? How shall we be fed? Who will receive us there?' With his tools on his back, so that he may earn his poor livelihood and that of his family in the sweat of his brow, he sets forth on his journey. How heavily this dejection and distress of mind, of which we have spoken, must have oppressed him, since the Angel had not told him how long a time he must remain in Egypt, and he could not settle down in any fixed abode, not knowing when he might be commanded to return.

"St. Paul (Heb. 11: 8, 9) greatly admired the obedience of Abraham, when God commanded him to leave his **country** (Gen. 12: 1) without telling him **in what direction he should go**. The Patriarch did not reply: 'Lord, Thou hast bid me go forth; tell me only if I shall pass through the South gate or through the North?' but instantly set out and went whither the Spirit of God conducted him. How much more shall we not admire the perfect obedience of St. Joseph! The Angel did not tell him how long he was to remain in Egypt, and he did not inquire. He remained there for the space of five years, as is generally believed, without asking any question as to his return, secure that He Who had commanded his departure would also command his return, and he remained ready always to obey the divine voice. He was in a land not only strange but hostile to the Israelites, inasmuch as the Egyptians resented the fact of their having escaped from their tyranny, and also of their having been the cause of many of their nation being drowned in the depths of the Red Sea, when in pursuit of them. I leave you, therefore, to imagine how great must have been St. Joseph's desire to return, on account of the continual fear in which he lived among the Egyptians. The anxiety, too, of not knowing when he might depart, must greatly have afflicted and tormented his poor heart. Yet he remained always himself, always gentle, tranquil, and persevering in his submission to the good pleasure of God, to Whose guidance he yielded implicitly, for as he was **a just man** (Matt. 1: 19), his will was always absolutely united and conformed to the Will of God.

"To be just is, indeed, to be perfectly united to the Divine Will, and to be always conformed to it in all sorts of events, whether prosperous or adverse. That St. Joseph was this, no one can doubt. See how the Angel moulds him like wax in his hands! He tells him that he must go into Egypt; he goes. He commands him to return into his own country; he returns. God wills that he should be always poor, which is one of the heaviest trials that He can lay upon him, and he submits lovingly not for a time only, but for his whole life. And what poverty — despised, rejected, needy poverty!

"That voluntary poverty which is one of the vows of Religious is very mild, since it does not prevent them from receiving and taking things necessary to them: forbidding and depriving them only of superfluities. But the poverty of St. Joseph, of Our Lord and of Our Lady, was not like this, for although it too was voluntary, and although they loved it dearly, it was nevertheless abject, mean, despised, and most needy; for everyone looked upon this Saint as a poor carpenter. (Matt. 13: 55; Mark 6: 3.) Though he toiled with the most affectionate zeal for the support of his little family, yet he could not earn enough to prevent their wanting many necessary things. Then, as the years went on, and his poverty and abjection continued, he still submitted always most humbly to the Will of God. He never allowed himself to be conquered or subdued by dejection of mind, which yet, no doubt, constantly attacked him, but always increased and grew in more perfect submission, as in all other virtues. So, too, it was with Our Lady, who day by day gained an increase of virtues and perfections from contact with her all-holy Son, Who Himself being unable to grow in any perfection — since He was, from the moment of His conception, what He is and will be eternally (Heb. 8: 8) — bestowed upon the Holy Family, of which He deigned to be a member, this grace of continual growth and advance in perfection. Our Lady drew hers from His own divine goodness, and St. Joseph received it, as we have said, through the intervention of Our Lady.

"What more remains to be said, except that we can never for a moment doubt that this glorious Saint has great influence in Heaven with Him Who raised him there in body and in soul — a fact which is the more probable because we have no relic of that body left to us here below! Indeed, it seems to me that no one can doubt this as a truth, for how could He Who had been so obedient to St. Joseph, all through His life, refuse him this grace? Doubtless when Our Lord descended into Limbo He was accosted by St. Joseph in words like these: 'Oh, my Lord, remember, if it please Thee, that when Thou didst come down from Heaven to earth, I received Thee into my house and my family, and that at the moment of Thy birth I received Thee into my arms. Now that Thou art returning to Heaven, take me there with Thee; I received Thee into my family, receive me now into Thine. I have carried Thee in my arms, take me into Thine; and as I carefully nourished and protected Thee in Thy mortal life, take care of me and lead me into life immortal'. And if it is true, as we are bound to believe, that in virtue of the Blessed Sacrament which we receive, our bodies will come to life again in the day of judgment (John 6: 55), how could we doubt that Our Lord raised up to Heaven, in body and soul, the glorious St. Joseph? For he had the honor and the grace of carrying Him so often in his blessed arms, those arms in which Our Lord took so much pleasure. Oh, how many and what tender kisses His sacred lips bestowed on him, to reward him for his toil and labors!

"St. Joseph is, then, undoubtedly in Heaven in body and soul. Oh, how happy shall we be if we can merit a share in his holy intercession! for nothing will be refused to him either by Our Lady or by her glorious Son. If we have confidence in him, he will obtain for us growth in all virtues, but especially in those which, as we have seen, he possesses in a higher degree than any other man. These are great purity of body and mind, humility, constancy, courage, and perseverance. These virtues will make us victorious in this life over our enemies, and through them we shall merit the grace to enjoy in eternal life the rewards prepared for those who shall imitate the example given by St. Joseph whilst in this life — a reward which will be nothing less than eternal happiness, in which we shall enjoy the unclouded vision of the Father, the Son, and the Holy Ghost. Blessed be God!"

* * *

St. Alphonsus Liguori

"The holy example of Jesus Christ Who, while upon earth, honored St. Joseph so highly and was obedient to Him during His life should be sufficient to inflame the hearts of all with devotion to this saint.

"Since we all must die, we should cherish a special devotion to St. Joseph that he may obtain for us a happy death. All Christians regard him as the advocate of the dying who assists at the hour of death those who honored him during their life, and that for three reasons:

"First, because Jesus Christ loved him not only as a friend but as a father, and on this account his mediation is far more efficacious than that of any other saint.

"Second, because St. Joseph has obtained special power against the evil spirits, who tempt us with redoubled vigor at the hour of death.

"Third, the assistance given St. Joseph at his death by Jesus and Mary obtained for him the right to secure a holy and peaceful death for his servants. Hence, if they invoke him at the hour of death he will not only help them, but he will also obtain for them the assistance of Jesus and Mary."

* * *

St. Bernardine of Siena

"If you compare St. Joseph to the whole Church of Christ is he not the special and chosen being of whom and under whom the Lord was introduced into the world with becoming dignity? If all the faithful are debtors to the Virgin Mother for being made worthy through her to receive the Redeemer, there can be no doubt that next to the

Mother of God we owe to St. Joseph our special homage and veneration."

* * *

Teresa of Avila

During an illness in which no earthly physician was able to give her relief, St. Teresa decided to implore the blessed in Heaven to restore her health. She writes: "I chose for my patron and lord the glorious St. Joseph, and I recommended myself earnestly to him. I saw that, both from this my present trouble, and from those of greater consequence relating to my honor and the loss of my soul, this my father and lord delivered me and rendered me greater services than I knew how to ask for. I **do not remember that I ever asked him at any time for anything which he did not obtain for me.** It fills me with amazement when I consider the numberless graces which God has granted me through the intercession of this blessed saint and the perils, both of body and soul, from which he has delivered me.

"To other saints the Most High seems to have given grace to succor men in some special necessity, but this glorious saint, I know by experience, has power to help us in all. Our Lord wishes us to understand by this that as He Himself was subject to St. Joseph while on earth, recognizing in him the authority of foster father and guardian, so now in

Heaven He is pleased to grant all his requests. Knowing by experience St. Joseph's astonishing influence with God, I would wish to persuade everyone to honor him with particular devotion. I have always seen those who honored him in a special manner make progress in virtue, for this heavenly protector favors in a striking manner the spiritual advancement of souls who commend themselves to him. For several years I have been accustomed to ask some favor on his feast, and I have always received it. If the petition be in any way amiss, he directs it aright for my greater welfare. If anyone does not believe it, I beg of him, for the love of God, to make the trial. He will see by experience how advantageous it is to commend himself to this glorious saint and to honor him with particular devotion.

"Those who are devoted to prayer should, in a special manner, cherish devotion to St. Joseph. I know not how anyone can ponder on the sufferings, trials and tribulations the Queen of Angels endured whilst caring for Jesus in His childhood, without at the same time thanking St. Joseph for the services he rendered the Divine Child and His Blessed Mother. Let him who cannot find anyone to teach him to pray, choose this glorious saint for his master, and he will not stray from the right path.

"Would that I could persuade all men to foster devotion to this glorious Saint because of the singular proof that I have of the many favors he obtains for us of God. I have never known a person to have been truly devoted to St. Joseph and to have rendered him special honor without seeing him advance rapidly in virtue; because the holy Patriarch assists with special care those who recommend themselves to him... Should the reader not believe my words, I only ask him for the love of God to make a trial and he will experience for himself what a grace it is to recommend oneself to this glorious Patriarch; but persons of prayer in particular should be especially devoted to him."

St. Teresa of Avila, Life, Baglioni, 1723, page 22.

* * *

St. Thomas Aquinas

"Some saints are privileged to extend to us their patronage with particular efficacy in certain needs, but not in others; but our holy patron, St. Joseph, has the power to assist us **in all cases, in every necessity, in every undertaking.**"

* * *

St. Madaleine Sophie Barat

"The two greatest personages who ever lived on this earth subjected themselves to him. Jesus wished to become indebted to St. Joseph for the necessaries of life, and of this holy Patriarch alone it may be said that he saved the life of his Savior. Let us love Jesus above all; let us love Mary as our Mother; but, then, how could we keep from loving Joseph, who was so intimately united to both Jesus and Mary? And how can we honor him better than by imitating his virtues? Now, what else did he do in all his life but contemplate, study and adore Jesus, even in the midst of his daily labors? Behold, therefore, our model."

* * *

Bl. Virgin Mary to St. Bridget of Sweden

"St. Joseph was so reserved and careful in his speech, that not one word ever issued from his mouth that was not good and holy, nor did he ever indulge in unnecessary or less charitable conversation. He was most patient and diligent in bearing fatigue; he practised extreme poverty; he was most meek in bearing injuries; he was strong and constant against my enemies; he was the faithful witness of the wonders of Heaven, being dead to the flesh and the world, living only for God and for heavenly goods, which were the only things he desired. He was perfectly conformed to the Divine Will and so resigned to the dispositions of Heaven, that he ever repeated: 'May the Will of God ever be done in me!' He rarely spoke with men, but continually with God, Whose Will he desired to perform. Wherefore, he now enjoys great glory in Heaven."

* * *

Pope Pius IX

"I have seen a little picture which represents St. Joseph with the divine Infant, Who points towards him, saying: 'Ite ad Joseph!' To you I say the same. Go to Joseph! Have recourse with special confidence to St. Joseph, for his protection is most powerful, as he is the patron of the universal Church."

* * *

St. Pierre Julien Eymard

"Our Lord has given me today a singular grace. He has inspired me to dedicate myself in an especial manner to St. Joseph as to my father, leader and protector.... He will be the spiritual director of my interior life, in order that I may lead that same life with him, hidden with Jesus and Mary and with his own self. I will imitate him especially in his silence regarding himself....

"I dedicated myself to St. Joseph as to my leader and master in all my duties as superior, so that I may fulfill these duties as I should, being meek and humble of heart as he himself was, endeavoring to be meek of heart with my brethren, humble with myself, and simple before God. I have chosen this good Saint to be my counselor and bosom friend. I have taken him for my protector in troubles and difficulties, and for the protector of my Congregation, as being the little family of Jesus. I have not asked him to free me from my crosses and trials, but only from that self-love which spoils them and turns them into arguments of vanity.

"I have prayed to Our Lord that He might give me St. Joseph for a father, as He had given me Mary for a mother; that he might put in my heart that devotion, that confidence, that filial love of a client, of a devotee of St. Joseph. I trust the good Master has heard my prayers, for I now feel greater devotion to this great Saint, and I am full of confidence and hope."

* * *

Bl. Virgin to Ven. Mary of Jesus of Agreda

"My daughter, although you have written that my spouse Joseph was one of the greatest saints and most noble princes of the celestial Jerusalem, you cannot now declare his eminent sanctity. Mortals can never know it until they enjoy the vision of God, in which they will with admiration discover the mystery, and they will praise the Lord for it. In the last day when all men will be judged, the unhappy damned will weep bitterly for not having known, because of their sins, this powerful and efficacious means for their salvation, and for not having availed themselves of it, as they could have done, to recover the grace of the just Judge. The world has been greatly ignorant of the magnitude of the prerogatives which the supreme Lord has accorded to my holy spouse, and how powerful is his intercession with His Divine Majesty; for be assured that he is one of the greatest favorites of God, and one of the most capable of appeasing His justice against sinners. I desire you to be most grateful to the goodness of the Lord for the favor which I have granted to you on this occasion, and that you will render Him continual thanks for the illumination that you have received touching this mystery. Endeavor also, in future, to augment your devotion for my holy spouse, and bless the Lord for that He has favored him with so much liberality, and also for the consolation that I enjoyed in bearing him company and knowing his perfections.

"You must avail yourself of his intercession in all your necessities, and so act as to multiply the numbers of his votaries. Recommend to your daughters to distinguish themselves in this devotion, since the Most High grants on earth that which my spouse requests in Heaven, and He will unite to these requests extraordinary favors for men, provided they do not render themselves unworthy to receive them.

"All these privileges respond to the perfection, the innocence, and to the eminent virtues of this admirable saint, because they have attracted the complaisance of the Lord, Who destines for him inconceivable largesses, and Who desires to show great mercy to those who will have recourse to his intercession."

* * *

St. Ephrem

"No one will ever be able worthily to praise Joseph, whom Thou, O true only-begotten Son of the Eternal Father, hast designed to have for Thy foster father!"

* * *

Our Lord to St. Margaret of Cortona

"I wish, O Margaret, to make known to thee how greatly the devotion thou hast to My foster father pleases Me; but I desire that every day thou wouldst render him whatever tribute of praise and honor thou canst, as he is most dear to My Heart."

* * *

Rev. Isidore Isolano, O. P., 16th century

"The Holy Ghost will never cease to act on the hearts of the faithful until the universal Church honors with transports the divine Joseph with a new veneration, founds monasteries, builds churches, erects altars in his name, multiplies his Feasts, and celebrates them more solemnly. The Lord will send His light into the inmost places of minds and hearts. Great men will scrutinize the interior gifts of God hidden in St. Joseph, and they will find in him a treasure of inestimable price. The riches and abundance of spiritual graces have shone with a brightness unique in his person, of such a kind that he cannot be compared either to the Saints of the Old Law or the New. . . .

"Bless then, O ye people, bless St. Joseph in order that you may be filled with benedictions, for whoever will bless him will be blessed with superabundant blessings. . . . We have every reason to believe that the immortal God wishes at the end of time to honor Joseph in the empire of the Church militant with honors most brilliant, and to render him the object of the most profound veneration."

MAN OF THE YEAR

"A terrible famine is laying waste to our world. It is not so much a famine of food, although millions are starving. Nor is it a famine of gold, for the world has too much of that and it has made us unhappy. Rather we are suffering from a famine of a more serious nature: and this is the famine of great men. As Bishop Sheen has written: 'The world today is suffering from a terrible nemesis of mediocrity. We are dying of ordinariness; we are perishing from our pettiness. The world's greatest need is great men'.

"The great magazines across America will soon be offering their pick of 'The Man of the Year'. Roving reporters will be on the lookout for a model to offer their readers; for a man who has carved a foothold in the solid granite of success. The editors ... will gather in plush offices to sift the world's celebrities. With news-hungry eyes they will scan the four corners of the earth in search of a great man. Some will choose a four-star general; others a popular athelete; still others a well-known industrialist or a public benefactor.

"But we will be a little disappointed with their choice. For we know that greatness does not consist in winning wars or in winning pennants. It does not consist in building airplanes or making money. It does not even consist in giving money away; nor in material success or achievement or in anything that strikes the eye. Our world needs great men of another calibre: men who are convinced that greatness is first and foremost a quality of the heart; men convinced that it is better to scale the ladder of sanctity than to scale Everest and plant the first flag on its snowy peaks; that it is better to avoid wars than to win them; that the greatest battles are won in the great fight against sin; men, finally who are really convinced that:

>'God greatness
>Flows around our incompleteness
>Round our restlessness, His rest.'

"These are the qualities that move the world. Indeed, in a very definite sense, these are the qualities that move Heaven, for they win the Heart of God. Therefore to the editors and reporters of America we present St. Joseph as our pick for **Man of the Year**. We offer him to a weary world as a model of real manhood, as a man who succeeded because he knew the secret of true greatness.

"It is customary to speak of a great man's message for our times. But Joseph has a thousand different messages for our times. He has, one might say, as many messages as there are ears to receive them. He has a message for the fathers and the husbands; for the teachers and the workmen. As uncrowned king of his nation, he can be counted upon to lend a helping-hand to the muddled political scene. His hidden life is the answer to the modern world's inordinate pride and false ambition. And in an age that spurns the ideal of sanctity, the man nearest to Christ will have a special communication.

As patron of a happy death, he is a constant source of hope in this era that so dreads the great beyond. As the peacemaker, he reminds a war-torn century of the ideal of the Beatitudes. As protector of the universal Church, he assures us that victory is ours in the bitter struggle against persecution.

"These and countless others are the messages of St. Joseph for our times. It would indeed be an understatement to speak of any single message. They are like the stars at night and the fishes in the sea: without number! The great silent Saint seems to cry out like a voice in the wilderness of the 20th century. The broad figure of the worker of Nazareth is rising out of the mists of obscurity and casting its shadow across the centuries.

"All of this fills us with great hope. For we believe that Joseph's era is breaking over the world like a new sunrise. He is taking things in hand and showing us the road to sane living. People are gradually coming to know this great Saint better; they are turning to him for the answer to their problems. They see in him the perfect portrait of true greatness. The night of our times has been long, it is true. Despair and discouragement are the landmarks of our day. Men's hearts have grown dry and desolate. But in some mysterious way God is preparing the conversion of the world. The facts leave no doubt that Joseph will play a leading role in this conversion. His message is like an aurora on the horizon, proclaiming a splendid day.

"There is an old saying that times of crisis are the test of greatness. It is certainly true in Joseph's case. Against the upheavals of our century, his greatness stands forth in bold relief. We are reminded of the lines of Longfellow:

> 'When a great man dies,
> For years beyond our ken,
> The light he leaves behind him lies
> Upon the paths of men!'

"Joseph has left his light upon our paths. His greatness has survived the ages. It goes beyond the years and towers up into the heavens. The one profound secret of his career — for a career it truly was — was the realization that all true achievement must be based on sanctity. In short, Joseph realized that the world's greatest need is saints, for saints are the greatest men. Because, therefore, of his sanctity — his silence, his love, his humility and his wisdom — he is our choice for **Man of the Year**."

Bernard Murchland, C. S. C., in "The Annals of St. Joseph of Mount Royal", Jan. 1954

LITURGICAL PRAISE OF ST. JOSEPH

THE DIVINE PRAISES

Blessed be God.
Blessed be His Holy Name.
Blessed be Jesus Christ, true God and true Man.
Blessed be the Name of Jesus.
Blessed be His Most Sacred Heart.
Blessed be His Most Precious Blood.
Blessed be Jesus in the Most Holy Sacrament of the Altar.
Blessed be the Holy Spirit, the Paraclete.
Blessed be the great Mother of God, Mary most holy.
Blessed be her Holy and Immaculate Conception.
Blessed be her Glorious Assumption.
Blessed be the name of Mary, Virgin and Mother.
Blessed be St. Joseph, her most chaste Spouse.
Blessed be God in His Angels and in His Saints.

O LUX BEATA COELITUM
POPE LEO XIII 1810-1903

O light that blesseth Saints above,
    O brightest hope of mortals here,
Jesus, on Whom domestic love
    Smiled, making childhood's home so dear.

O Mary, with rich graces blest,
    Who gav'st, as only thou couldst do,
To Jesus' lips a virgin breast,
    And with thy milk thy kisses too.

And thou, from Israel's fathers ta'en,
    The Virgin's guardian called to be,
Her Child Divine, not all in vain,
    The sweet name, father, gave to thee.

You, come of Jesse's noble stem,
    Salvation brought to every land,
Then hearken to the prayer of them
    Who here before your altar stand.

Now, while the sun toward evening dips,
    And beauty takes from things away,
Here lingering rises to our lips
    All that our inmost hearts would say.

Where'er your home, your virtues bore,
    With every grace, its fairest flowers;
So may we flourish evermore
    In this domestic life of ours.

Jesus, Who an obedient Son
    Unto Thy parents willed to be,
With Father and with Spirit one,
    Be glory evermore to Thee.

SACRA JAM SPLENDENT DECORATA LYCHINIS
POPE LEO XIII

Now lamps our churches flood with light,
Now altars gleam with garlands bright,
Now censers, in sweet odors, raise
    Their precious praise.

'Twere sweet to sing, and well 'twere done,
The royal birth of God's own Son,
Or David's ancient line, and see
    God's ancestry.

But sweeter Nazareth's lowly cot
To praise, and Jesus' humble lot;
Or tell in words with sweetness rife
    His silent life.

Quick, Angel-led, from Nile's far shore
The wanderer is home once more:
The Boy, Who evil days has passed,
    Is safe at last.

To youth grows Jesus, day by day
Passing His hidden life away,
And wills to learn, with Joseph's aid,
    His lowly trade.

"Toil", said He, "well may make Me sweat,
Who one day will with Blood be wet:
Let this pain, too, cleanse, for it can,
    Poor, sinful man."

The Mother sits her Son beside,
Near Joseph strays his Virgin-Bride,
Their happy handmaid, making less
    Their weariness.

You Three, who toil and suffering knew,
The wretched aid who turn to you,
But help them most who most endure,
    The struggling poor.

Strip men of pride whose wealth is spent
On pleasure; and make us content:
Toward all who pray for strength incline,
    With eyes benign.

Praise to Thee, Jesus, Who didst give
The laws whereby true life we live —
With Father throned and Holy Ghost,
    Mid Heaven's host.

O GENTE FELIX HOSPITA
POPE LEO XIII

O happy and august abode
    That once made Nazareth so blest,
The infant Church its nurture owed
    To thy most hospitable breast.

The sun that, with its golden light,
    Wide o'er the earth so loves to roam,
Has never seen so sweet a sight
    As this delightful, holy home.

Here from the palace of the sky,
    Flock messengers on frequent wing;
They come, and come again, thereby
    The shrine of virtue honoring.

With ready hand, and right goodwill,
    Doth Jesus Joseph's wishes do:
How Mary doth, with rapturous thrill,
    A mother's household tasks pursue!

Joseph is near his spouse; and he
    In all her love and care partakes:
The Source of virtue graciously
    'Twixt them a thousand love-ties makes.

They mutually loving, turn
    Their loves to Jesus, both in one;
And, making both their bosoms burn,
    His love rewards their unison.

May charity, that ne'er will cease,
    Between us, too, firm bonds create,
And, fostering thus, domestic peace,
    Life, life so hard, alleviate.

Jesus, Who an obedient Son
    Unto Thy parents willed to be,
With Father and with Spirit one,
    Be glory evermore to Thee.

TE, JOSEPH, CELEBRANT
17TH CENTURY

Joseph, to tell thy praise, let all the Angels sing;
Let quiring Christendom their songs of thee repeat;
The glorious Virgin's spouse who merited to be
    In virgin wedlock sweet.

When, as her gracious Fruit was growing day by day,
Thy soul in sore amaze now this, now that believed,
An Angel, whispering, said that by the Holy Ghost
    Her Babe had been conceived.

Thy arms thy new-born Lord most lovingly enfold;
Thou fleest as He flees to Egypt's alien shore;
Thou in Jerusalem, when He is lost, dost find,
    And grief turns joy once more.

We, only after death, the heavenly palm obtain;
But thou in life wert made the peer of Saints above:
Thy happier lot it was thy God on earth to see
    And love with wondering love.

Be clement to our prayer, O Trinity supreme!
Grant us, for Joseph's sake, the starry heights to scale;
That of Thy Name at last, in songs of gratitude,
    Our praise may never fail.

COELITUM JOSEPH
17th century

Joseph, the glory of the Saints in Heaven,
Life's certain hope, and of the world a pillar,
Graciously hear the songs of praise thy clients
    Joyfully sing thee.

Spouse of the spotless Virgin the Creator
Made thee, and willed that of His Word the father,
Thou shouldst be called, appointing thee to serve Him
    Toward our salvation.

Yes, the Redeemer lying in a stable,
Who was to come, as sang the songs of Prophets,
Gladly thou seest, Godhead in that Infant
    Humbly adoring.

God, King of kings, and Lord of all creation,
He, at Whose nod the hordes infernal tremble,
He, Whom the prostrate Heavens are ever serving
    Was subject to thee.

Praise never-ending to the Triune Godhead,
Who, in such wise, hath honored thee supremely:
May He vouchsafe to grant us, through thy merits
    Bliss with the Blessed.

ISTE, QUEM LAETI
17th century

Joseph, whom gladly we, the faithful, honor,
Hymning the praise of so sublime a triumph
This very day once merited to enter
    Bliss everlasting.

Happy, thrice happy, blessed, oh! thrice blessed
He who, when mortal life was near its ending,
Jesus and Mary had, to watch beside him,
    Smiling serenely.

Hell overcoming thus, from flesh unfettered,
Calm and in slumber, to his home eternal
Lo! he has passed, about his brow entwining
    Glorious garlands.

Then, let us beg him, from his throne in Heaven
Hither to come and, for our faults and failings
Pardon obtaining, grant us peace supernal,
    Gifted so greatly.

Glory and praise be Thine, O Thou, the Triune,
O'er us Who reignest as our God, and crownest
Servants found faithful with Thy crowns all golden,
    Splendid forever.

PAPAL PRAISE OF ST. JOSEPH

The first modern pronouncement concerning St. Joseph was made by Pope Pius IX, on December 8, 1870, when he placed the entire Catholic Church under the patronage of St. Joseph with the title of Patron of the Universal Church. The following is the **Decree for the City and the World:***

"As Almighty God appointed Joseph, son of the Patriarch Jacob, over all the land of Egypt to save grain for the people, so when the fulness of time was come and He was about to send on earth His only-begotten Son, the Savior of the world, He chose another Joseph of whom the first Joseph had been the type, and whom He made the lord and chief of His household and possessions, the guardian of His choicest treasures. So also He espoused to Himself the Immaculate Virgin Mary, and of her was born, by the Holy Spirit, Jesus Christ our Lord, Who in the sight of men deigned to be reputed the son of Joseph, and was subject to him. And so it was that Him, Whom countless Kings and Prophets had of old desired to see, Joseph not only saw but conversed with, and embraced in paternal affection, and kissed, and most sedulously nourished

---

*This and the following Papal documents are taken from *The Man Nearest to Christ* by F. L. Filas, S. J., — The Bruce Pub. Co., Milwaukee.

— even Him Whom the faithful were to receive as the Bread that came down from Heaven whereby they might obtain eternal life.

"Because of this sublime dignity which God conferred on His most faithful servant the Church has always most highly honored and praised Blessed Joseph next to his spouse, the Virgin Mother of God, and has besought his intercession in times of trouble. And now, therefore, when in these most troublous times the Church is beset by enemies on every side and is weighed down by calamities so heavy that ungodly men imagine the gates of hell have at length prevailed against her, the venerable Prelates of the Catholic world have presented to the Sovereign Pontiff their own petitions and those of the faithful committed to their charge, praying that he would vouchsafe to constitute St. Joseph Patron of the Universal Church. And this their prayer and desire was renewed by them even more earnestly at the Sacred Ecumenical Council of the Vatican. Accordingly, now it has pleased our most holy Sovereign, Pius IX, Pope, deeply affected by the recent deplorable events, to comply with the desires of the prelates and to commit to St. Joseph's most powerful patronage himself and all the faithful. He therefore has declared St. Joseph Patron of the Universal Church, and has commanded that his festival, occurring on the 19th day of March, be celebrated for the future as a Double of the First Class, but without an octave, since it falls within the season of Lent.

"Finally, he has ordained that on this day, sacred to the Blessed Virgin Mother of God and to her most chaste spouse St. Joseph, a declaration to that effect, made by this present decree of the Congregation of Sacred Rites, be published."

* * *

The Congregation of Sacred Rites issued another decree on July 7, 1871, in which Pope Pius IX formally complemented the liturgical honors given St. Joseph.

"The Catholic Church rightly honors with its highest cultus and venerates with a feeling of deep reverence the illustrious Patriarch Blessed Joseph, now crowned with glory and honor in Heaven, whom Almighty God, in preference to all His saints, willed to be the chaste and true spouse of the Immaculate Virgin Mary as well as the foster-father of His only-begotten Son. Him also He enriched and filled to overflowing with graces entirely unique, enabling him to execute most faithfully the duties of a state so sublime. Wherefore, the Roman Pontiffs, Our Predecessors — in order that they might daily increase and more ardently stimulate in the hearts of the Christian faithful a reverence and devotion for the holy Patriarch, and that further they might exhort them to implore with the utmost confidence his intercession with God — have not failed to decree for him new and ever greater tokens of public veneration whenever the occasion served.

"Among these let it suffice to call to mind Our Predecessors of happy memory, Sixtus IV, who wished the Feast of St. Joseph to be inserted in the Roman Missal and Breviary; Gregory XV, who by a decree of May 8, 1621, ordered that the Feast should be observed in the whole world under a double precept; Clement X, who on December 6, 1670, accorded to the Feast the rite of a double of the second class; Clement XI, who by a decree of February 4, 1714, adorned the Feast with a complete Proper Mass and Office; and finally Benedict XIII, who by a decree published on December 19, 1726, ordered the name of the holy Patriarch to be added to the Litany of the Saints. And so, too, We Ourselves, raised to the supreme Chair of Peter by the inscrutable design of God, and moved by the example of Our illustrious Predecessors as well as by the singular devotion which from youth itself We entertained toward the holy Patriarch, have by a Decree of September 10, 1847, extended with great joy of soul the Feast of his Patronage to the whole Church, under the rite of Double of the

Second Class — a Feast which was already being celebrated in many places by a special indult of the Holy See.

"However, in these latter times, in which a monstrous and most abominable war has been declared against the Church of Christ, the devotion of the faithful toward St. Joseph has grown and progressed to such an extent that from every direction innumerable and fervent petitions have once more reached Us. These were recently renewed during the Sacred Ecumenical Council of the Vatican by all groups of the faithful and — what is more important — by many of Our Venerable Brethren, the Cardinals and Bishops of the Holy Roman Church. In their petitions they begged of Us that in these mournful days, as a safeguard against the evils which disturb us on every side, We should more efficaciously implore the compassion of God through the merits and intercession of St. Joseph, declaring him Patron of the Universal Church. Accordingly, moved by these requests, and after having invoked the Divine light, We deemed it right that so many and such pious desires should be granted. Hence, by a special Decree of Our Congregation of Sacred Rites — which We ordered to be proclaimed during High Mass in Our Patriarchal Basilicas of the Lateran, the Vatican, and the Liberian, on December 8, of the past year 1870, the holyday of the Immaculate Conception of his spouse — We solemnly declared the Blessed Patriarch Joseph Patron of the Universal Church, and We ordered that his Feast occurring on the 19th day of March should henceforth be celebrated in the whole world under the rite of a Double of the First Class, yet without an octave on account of Lent.

"Now, after our Declaration of the Holy Patriarch as Patron of the Universal Church, We think it but proper that in the public veneration of the Church each and every privilege of honor should be accorded him which belongs to special Patron Saints according to the general rubrics of the Roman Breviary and Missal. Therefore, after consultation with Our Venerable Brethren, the Cardinals of the Holy Roman Church who are entrusted with the supervision of the sacred rites, We, confirming and also amplifying with Our present Letters the aforesaid regulation of that Decree, command and enjoin the following:

"We desire that the **Credo** be always added in the Mass on the natal feast of St. Joseph as well as on the Feast of his Patronage, even though these feasts should occur on some day other than Sunday. Moreover, we desire that in the Oration **A Cunctis**, whenever it is to be recited, the commemoration of St. Joseph shall be added in the following words, 'with Blessed Joseph' — to be introduced after the invocation of the Blessed Virgin Mary and before all other Patron Saints, with the exception of the Angels and of St. John the Baptist. Finally, we desire that, while this order is to be observed in the Suffrages of the Saints whenever they are prescribed by the rubrics, the following commemoration should be added in honor of St. Joseph:

"**The Antiphons at Vespers**: Behold the faithful and prudent servant whom the Lord has set over His household. Glory and riches are in His house. And His justice remains for ever and ever.

"**The Antiphons at Lauds**: Jesus Himself, when He began His work, was about thirty years of age, being — as was supposed — the son of Joseph. The mouth of the just man shall meditate wisdom. And his tongue shall speak judgment.

"**The Oration**: O God, Who in Thine ineffable providence was pleased to choose blessed Joseph as the spouse of Thy most holy mother, grant, we beseech Thee, that we may be made worthy to have him for our intercessor in Heaven whom on earth we venerate as our protector.

"Given in Rome at St. Peter's, under the Seal of the Fisherman, July 7, 1871, the Twenty-sixth Year of Our Pontificate."

✻ ✻ ✻

Pope Leo XIII issued his Encyclical Letter, **Quamquam Pluries**, on August 15, 1889, in which he calls attention to the grievous anti-Catholic and

anti-Christian influence of his times, and the necessity of imploring the help of Mary, and of St. Joseph, who in dignity is second only to our Lady.
"Venerable Brethren:

Health and Apostolic Blessing.

"Although We have already ordered on several occasions that special prayers should be offered throughout the whole world and that Catholic interests should be recommended to God in a more earnest manner, let it not seem surprising to anyone if at this time We judge that this duty should be again called to mind. In difficult times, particularly when it seems that the 'powers of darkness' are able to make daring attempts to ruin the Christian name, the Church has always been accustomed to call humbly upon God, her founder and champion, with greater earnestness and perseverance. In such times she has sought aid also from the saints who dwell in Heaven, and principally from the august Virgin Mother of God, by whose patronage she knows that support in her trials will chiefly be afforded: for the fruit of such pious prayers and of hope in the Divine bounty will sooner or later become manifest.

"Now, Venerable Brethren, you have learned to understand the present age, hardly less calamitous to the Christian commonwealth than the very worst the world has hitherto experienced. Around us we behold faith, the foundation of all Christian virtues, perishing almost everywhere; we see charity waxing cold; youth growing up corrupted in morals and in doctrine; the Church of Jesus Christ attacked on every side with violence and rage, and a vicious war waged against the Papacy. We behold, in fact, the very groundwork of religion overthrown by assaults that increase in violence from day to day. As for the depths of this catastrophe of our age, and the ulterior schemes of agitators, you yourselves know more than it behooves Us to put into words.

"Amid such difficult and lamentable conditions the evils of our day have grown too great for human remedies. The only course left open is to seek a total cure through the Divine power. Because of this, therefore, We deemed it advisable to call upon the piety of the Faithful that they may implore the aid of Almighty God with greater earnestness and perseverance. But, particularly, with the month of October now approaching — which elsewhere We have decreed should be dedicated to the Virgin Mary of the Rosary — We urgently exhort that during the present year the entire month be spent in the greatest possible devotion and piety. We know that a refuge for us is ever ready in the material bounty of the Virgin; and with no less certainty we know that our hopes in her are not in vain. If she has come a hundred times to aid the Christian commonwealth in times of need, why should we doubt that she will give new examples of her power and favor provided that humble and continued public prayers are offered? Assuredly, we believe that she will help us all the more wonderfully the longer the period is during which she desires us to importune her.

"But still another proposal remains to be made, Venerable Brethren, well aware as We are that you will diligently cooperate with Us here as you have always done in the past. In order, then, that God may show Himself more willing to grant our petitions and that He may aid His Church more promptly and bountifully in proportion as more numerous voices are raised to Him, We have deemed it highly expedient that the Faithful should become accustomed to implore with special piety and trust the aid of the Virgin Mother of God, associating with this devotion their supplication for the aid of her most chaste spouse, Blessed Joseph. Indubitable evidence exists for us to conclude that such a method of approach will be desirable and pleasing to the Virgin herself.

"And in this connection, concerning which We are about to make Our first public pronouncement, We are aware that the piety of the people is not only favorably inclined but is advancing, as it were along a course already entered upon. For in times past the endeavor of the Roman Pontiffs had been gradually to extend the veneration of Joseph farther and farther, and to propagate it widely. In these latter days, however, We have seen that same veneration taking on everywhere unquestionably new stature, particularly after Our Predecessor, Pius IX of happy memory, conformably with the requests of numerous Bishops, had declared this holy Patriarch the Patron of the Universal Church. But precisely because it is highly advantageous that veneration for him be deeply rooted in Catholic morals and practices, We desire that the Faithful be moved thereto no less by Our own voice and authority.

"There are special reasons why Blessed Joseph should be explicitly named the Patron of the Church and why the Church should in turn expect much from his patronage and guardianship. For he, indeed, was the husband of Mary and the father, as was supposed, of Jesus Christ. From this arise all his dignity, grace, holiness, and glory. The dignity of the Mother of God is certainly so sublime that nothing can surpass it; but none the less, since the bond of marriage existed between Joseph and the Blessed Virgin, there can be no doubt that more than any other person he approached that supereminent dignity by which the Mother of God is raised far above all created natures. For marriage is the closest possible union and relationship whereby each spouse mutually participates in the goods of the other. Consequently, if God gave Joseph as a spouse to the Virgin, He assuredly gave him not only as a companion in life, a witness of her virginity, and the guardian of her honor, but also as a sharer in her exalted dignity by reason of the conjugal tie itself. Likewise, Joseph alone stands out in august dignity because he was the guardian of the Son of God by the Divine appointment, and in the opinion of men was His father. As a consequence the Word of God was modestly obedient to Joseph, was attentive to his commands, and paid to him every honor that children should render their parent.

"From this double dignity, moreover, such duties arose as are prescribed by nature for the head of a household. Joseph was at once the legitimate and the natural guardian, preserver, and defender of the Divine household over which he presided. Zealously he watched over his spouse and her Divine offspring with the most ardent love and constant solicitude. By his labor he regularly provided for both of them such necessities of life as food and clothing. In seeking a place of refuge he warded off that danger to their lives which had been engendered by the jealousy of a king. Amid the inconveniences of the journey and the bitterness of exile, he continually showed himself the companion, the helper, the consoler of the Virgin and of Jesus.

"Moreover, the Divine household, which Joseph governed as with paternal authority, contained the beginnings of the new Church. The Virgin most holy is the mother of all Christians since she is the mother of Jesus and since she gave birth to them on the mount of Calvary amid the unspeakable sufferings of the Redeemer. Jesus is, as it were, the first born of Christians, who are His brothers by adoption and redemption. From these considerations we conclude that the Blessed Patriarch must regard all the multitude of Christians who constitute the Church as confided to his care in a certain special manner. This is his numberless family, scattered throughout all lands, over which he rules with a sort of paternal authority, because he is the husband of Mary and the father of Jesus Christ. Thus, it is conformable to reason, and in every way becoming to Blessed Joseph, that as once it was his sacred trust to guard with watchful care the family at Nazareth, no matter what befell, so now, by virtue of his heavenly patronage, he is in turn to protect and to defend the Church of Christ.

"The statements here made, Venerable Brethren, as you will readily perceive, are confirmed by what We shall further set forth. Conformably, namely, with the Church's sacred liturgy, the opinion has been held by not a few Fathers of the Church that the ancient Joseph, son of the patriarch Jacob, foreshadowed both in person and office our own St. Joseph. By his glory he was a prototype of the grandeur of the future guardian of the Holy Family. In addition to the circumstance that both men bore the same name — a name by no means devoid of significance — it is well known to you that they resembled each other very closely in other ways as well. Notable in this regard are the facts that the earlier Joseph received special favor and benevolence from his lord, and that, when placed by him as ruler over his household, fortune and prosperity abundantly accrued to the master's house because of Joseph.

"There was even a more evident similarity when by the king's order he was given supreme power over the entire kingdom. When calamity brought on a deficient harvest and a scarcity of grain, he exercised such excellent foresight in behalf of the Egyptians and their neighbors that the king decreed he should be styled 'savior of the world'. Thus, in that ancient patriarch we may recognize the distinct image of St. Joseph. As the one was prosperous and successful in the domestic concerns of his lord and in an exceptional manner was set over the whole kingdom, so the other, destined to guard the name of Christ, could well be chosen to defend and to protect the Church, which is truly the house of God and the kingdom of God on earth.

"This is the reason why all the faithful of all places and conditions commend and confide themselves to the guardianship of Blessed Joseph. In Joseph, fathers of families have an eminent model of paternal care and providence. Married couples find in him the perfect image of love, harmony, and conjugal loyalty. Virgins can look to him for their pattern and as the guardian of virginal integrity. With the picture of Joseph set before them, those of noble lineage can learn to preserve their dignity even under adverse circumstances. Let the wealthy understand what goods they should chiefly seek and earnestly amass, while with no less special right the needy, the laborers, and all possessed of merely modest means should fly to his protection and learn to imitate him. Joseph was of royal blood; he was espoused to the greatest and the holiest of all womankind; he was the father, as was supposed, of the Son of God; yet none the less, he devoted his life to labor, and by his hands and skill produced whatever was necessary for those dependent on him.

"Therefore, if truth be sought, the condition of those reduced to slender means is not disgraceful. The labor of craftsmen far from being dishonorable, can by virtue be even greatly ennobled. Joseph, content with what was his own, little as it doubtless was, bore with calm and dignified spirit the straitened circumstances necessarily connected with his meager means of livelihood. This was conformable to the example of his Son, Who having accepted the form of a servant, while being Lord of all, willingly subjected Himself to the utmost indigence and poverty. Considerations such as these will serve to encourage and tranquillize the poor and all those who live by the labor of their hands. Nevertheless, although it is permitted them to rise from a condition of want to one of well-being, provided violation of justice is excluded, yet both justice and reason forbid the destruction of that order which Divine Providence has ordained. On the contrary, it is foolish to have recourse to violence, and to seek to better existing conditions by sedition and revolt, which in most cases produce only greater evils than those which they were meant to cure. If the poor wish to act wisely, let them not believe the promises of seditious men, but let them trust in the example and patronage of St. Joseph, and in the maternal care of the Church, which daily becomes more solicitous for their welfare.

"Accordingly, Venerable Brethren, relying mainly on your episcopal authority and zeal, and confidence that the truly good and pious will of their own desire and volition perform more numerous and signal acts than such merely as are demanded of them, We decree that during the month of October, a prayer to St. Joseph shall be added to the recitation of the Rosary.

"Concerning the Rosary, we have elsewhere already legislated, but a copy of the prayer to St. Joseph is sent to you along with these Letters. We decree that this order shall be observed in future years in perpetuity. To those who shall piously recite this prayer, We grant them singly an indulgence of seven years and seven quarantines for each recitation.

"Salutary and deserving of highest commendation is the practice of consecrating the month of March by daily exercises of piety in honor of the holy Patriarch. That indeed has already been observed in many places. But wherever it cannot readily be accomplished, We desire that, preceding the Feast of St. Joseph, a triduum of prayers should be held in the principal church of each city. In localities where the 19th of March, sacred to Blessed Joseph, is not included among the feasts of obligation, We exhort all voluntarily to keep holy this day by private exercises of devotion in honor of our heavenly Patron, and to do this with the same zeal as if they were obeying a precept.

"Meanwhile, as a promise of heavenly favors and as a testimony of Our benevolence toward you,

Venerable Brethren, and toward your clergy and your people, We most lovingly bestow on you the Apostolic Blessing in the Lord.

<small>"Given at Rome at St. Peter's, the 15th day of August, 1889, the Twelfth Year of Our Pontificate."</small>

* * *

On page 73 of this work we have quoted from the Apostolic Brief of Pope Leo XIII (**Neminem Fugit**), in which he states that St. Joseph participated intimately in the supreme dignity of the Holy Family — the model for all Christian families.

* * *

Fifty years after St. Joseph had been proclaimed Patron of the Universal Church by Pope Pius IX, Pope Benedict XV, in 1920, selected him as the patron of workmen.

"Good and salutary indeed it was for the Christian people that Our Predecessor, Pius IX of immortal memory, solemnly declared the most chaste spouse of the Virgin Mary and guardian of the Incarnate Word, St. Joseph, to be the Patron of the Universal Church. But now that the fiftieth anniversary of this happy event will occur next December, We consider it useful and opportune that it should be worthily celebrated by the whole Catholic world.

"Casting Our glance over the past fifty years, We behold the wonderfully flourishing condition of pious institutions which bear witness to the manner in which devotion to the holy Patriarch has been gradually developing among the Faithful. When further, then, We consider the calamities afflicting the human race today, we cannot fail to realize how opportune it is to increase this devotion and to spread it ever more widely throughout Christian peoples.

"In Our Encyclical, "On the Reconciliation of Christian Peace", following the cruel war, We indicated what was necessary to establish order and tranquillity everywhere. In particular consideration was given by Us to the civil relations which exist between nations and between individuals. Yet today the treatment of another cause of disturbance, much more serious, becomes imperative. There is question now of an evil that has crept into the very heart of society. For the scourge of war had been laid on the human race at the very moment that it had become profoundly infected with naturalism — that great worldly plague which, wherever it enters, lessens the desire for heavenly things, extinguishes the flame of Divine Love, and deprives man of the healing and elevating grace of Christ, leaving him without the light of faith, dependent on the weak and corrupt resources of nature and the slave of unbridled human passion. Thus it happened that many devoted themselves solely to the acquisition of worldly goods. Moreover, while the contest between the wealthy and the proletariat had already become acute, class hatred now became still more grave by reason of the length and severity of the War, for while this, on the one hand, brought intolerable privation to the masses, on the other it rapidly made fortunes for the few.

"Then, too, the sanctity of conjugal fidelity and respect for paternal authority were often grievously transgressed during the War. The remoteness of one spouse served to relax the duty to the other, and the absence of a watchful eye gave rise to freer and more indulgent conduct. More particularly was this notable among the younger women. Sincerely to be regretted, therefore, is the fact that public morals have become far more corrupt and depraved than they had previously been, and for this very reason, too, the so-called 'social question' has reached an intensity which causes one to fear the gravest evils.

"In the wishful thought and expectations of the seditious members of society there has consequently been maturing the advent of a certain universal commonwealth that is to be founded on absolute equality of men and on community of goods. National distinctions are no longer to exist in this, nor is any recognition to be given to the authority of the father over his sons, of public power over the citizens, or of God over men united in civil commonwealth. All such ravings, should they be carried into effect, must culminate in a tremendous social convulsion, such in fact as is now experienced and felt by not a small part of Europe. Precisely a similar condition of affairs, We are aware, is ambitioned among other peoples. The masses are wrought into excitement by the fury and audacity of a few, while grave disturbances break out in many places.

"Meanwhile, pre-occupied above all else with this course of events, We have not failed to renew in the sons of the Church a sense of their duty, whenever the occasion presented itself. This purpose, for example, We but recently accomplished through the letters addressed by Us to the Bishop of Bergamo and also to the Bishops of the Venetian Province. And so now, prompted by the same motive — namely, to recall to their duty those of our own fold, however many, who earn their bread by the labor of their hands, and to preserve them immune from the contagion of Socialism, than which nothing is more opposed to Christian wisdom — We have with great solicitude placed before them in a particular manner the example of St. Joseph, that they may follow him as their special guide and may honor him as their heavenly patron.

"It was he who, in very deed, lived a life similar to theirs; and for this reason Our Lord Jesus Christ, though in truth the only-begotten Son of the Eternal Father, wished to be called the 'son of the carpenter'. Yet how many and how great were the virtues with which he adorned his poor and humble condition! And among all these virtues none was wanting to ennoble the man who was to be the husband of Mary Immaculate and the foster-father of Our Lord Jesus Christ. Let all persons, then, learn from Joseph to consider present passing affairs in the light of future good which will endure forever; and final consolation amid human vicissitudes in the hope of heavenly things, that so they may aspire to them in a manner conformable to the Divine Will — that is, by living soberly, justly, and piously.

"In reference to the labor problem it is opportune to quote here the words which Our Predecessor, Leo XIII of happy memory, uttered on this question, for they are such that no other words can be considered appropriate:

'Considerations such as these will serve to encourage and tranquillize the poor and all those who live by the labor of their hands. Yet, although it is permitted them to rise from a condition of want to one of well-being, provided violation of justice is excluded, nevertheless, both justice and reason forbid the destruction of that order which Divine Providence has ordained. On the contrary, it is foolish to have recourse to violence, and to seek to better existing conditions by sedition and revolt, which in most cases produce only greater evils than those which they were meant to cure. If the poor wish to act wisely, let them not believe the promises of seditious men, but let them trust in the example and patronage of St. Joseph and in the maternal care of the Church, which daily becomes more solicitous for their welfare'.

"With the increase of devotion to St. Joseph among the faithful there will necessarily result an increase in their devotion toward the Holy Family of Nazareth of which he was the august head, for these devotions spring spontaneously one from the other. By St. Joseph we are led directly to Mary, and by Mary to the fountain of all holiness, Jesus Christ, Who sanctified the domestic virtues by His obedience toward St. Joseph and Mary.

"We desire, then, that these marvelous exemplars of virtue should serve as inspiration and as models for all Christian families. Even as the family constitutes the foundation of the human race, so by strengthening domestic society with the bonds of purity, fidelity, and concord, a new vigor, and, as it were, a new lifeblood shall be diffused through all the members of human society under the vivifying influence of the virtue of Christ; nor shall the result consist merely in the correction of public morals but in the restoration of public and civil discipline itself.

"Therefore, full of confidence in the patronage of him to whose providence and vigilance it pleased God to entrust His only-begotten Son as well as the Virgin most holy, We earnestly exhort all the Bishops of the Catholic world that in the Church's present need they should induce the faithful to implore more earnestly the powerful intercession of St. Joseph. And since there are many ways approved by this Apostolic See for venerating the holy Patriarch, especially on all Wednesdays of the year and during the month consecrated to him, We wish that at the instance of each Bishop all of these devotions should be practised in each diocese as far as possible.

"And then, too, since Joseph, whose death took place in the presence of Jesus and Mary, is justly regarded as the most efficacious protector of the dying, it is Our purpose here to lay a special injunction on Our Venerable Brethren that they assist in every possible manner those pious associations which have been instituted to obtain the intercession of St. Joseph for the dying — such as the 'Association for a Happy Death' and the 'Pious Union of St. Joseph's Passing', established for the benefit of those who are in their last agony.

"To commemorate the above Pontifical Decree We order and enjoin that within a year from the 8th of December next, throughout the whole Catholic world there shall be celebrated in honor of St. Joseph, Patron of the Universal Church, a solemn function at whatever time and in whatever manner each Bishop shall consider fitting; and to all who assist We grant a plenary indulgence under the usual conditions.

"Given at St. Peter's at Rome, July 25th, Feast of St. James the Apostle, 1920, in the Sixth Year of Our Pontificate."

* * *

On March 19, 1937, the Feast of St. Joseph, Pope Pius XI's Encyclical Letter (Divini Redemptoris), "On Atheistic Communism", was promulgated. Its concluding paragraphs declared St. Joseph to be the patron of the struggle against atheistic communism:

"To hasten the advent of that 'peace of Christ in the kingdom of Christ' so ardently desired by all, We place the vast campaign of the Church against world Communism under the standard of St. Joseph, her mighty Protector. He belongs to the working-class, and he bore the burdens of poverty for himself and the Holy Family, whose tender and vigilant head he was. To him was entrusted the Divine Child when Herod loosed his assassins against Him. In a life of faithful performance of everyday duties, he left an example for all those who must gain their bread by the toil of their hands. He won for himself the title of 'The Just', serving thus as a living model of that Christian justice which should reign in social life.

"With eyes lifted on high, Our Faith sees the new heavens and the new earth described by Our first Predecessor, St. Peter. While the promises of the false prophets of this earth melt away in blood and tears, the great apocalyptic prophecy of the Redeemer shines forth in heavenly splendor: 'Behold, I make all things new' ".

PART IV

Legends of St. Joseph

THE ROD IN BLOSSOM

Around the sacred ark the sons of Juda stand,
Sending to Heaven above their humble, fervent prayer;
What hath brought unto the temple the young men of the land,
And wherefore in each hand a wither'd branch and bare?

But yester eve, with joyous, hopeful heart,
They laid upon the altar each dry and mystic rod;
And sadly now they gaze, and their fondest hopes depart —
The branches still are leafless, no change hath come from God!

Behold them once again praying the Lord Most High;
But one, before unseen, has join'd their band —
One in whom calm and brightly-beaming eye
Are imaged virtues heroic and grand.

Lofty is his brow, majestic and serene;
He, too, doth in his hand a dry branch bear
Seeming the while amazed that he hath been
Call'd to contest a prize so passing rare.

Humble he is, although of lineage high,
Deeming himself, of all, the least and last,
And matchless pure in heart, wherefore th' all-seeing Eye
Hath been on him with special favor cast.

"Joseph, draw near!" from God the high-priest speaks,
And Joseph, in his turn, lays down his rod.
Oh, wondrous prodigy! full soon it breaks
Forth into leaves and flow'rs — all praise to God!

O Joseph, son of David! hail, all hail!
Thou art the favor'd one, the virgin thine —
The Virgin whose bright name shall never pale,
Who crushes Satan's head with power divine!

Thine is that lily fair, that spotless dove,
That fragrant flower that bloom'd for Eden's bow'rs,
The Lord hath chosen thee, with special love,
To guard His fairest one of all earth's flow'rs!

Favor'd art thou, and lo! thy destined bride,
Bright as the stars and more than heavenly pure,
Comes forth, the Lord with her, and at thy side
Receives the ring that makes the compact sure.

Hail then, chaste spouse of Mary, hail, thrice hail!
For Heaven, in giving her a spouse like thee,
So pure, so God-like, surely will not fail
To make thee our Protector, too, to be!

THE CHOSEN MAN

Mayhap 'tis but a legend
    The ancient writers tell,
That in God's Holy Temple
    Your rod began to swell
And burst to lily blossoms,
    To prove God's wondrous plan
That for the Virgin Mother
    He chose you Husbandman.

Or fact or legend be it,
    A greater truth was there
Though only Virgin Mary
    Beheld the vision fair.

She saw in your soul's garden
    The virgin lilies stand,
And knew God made you worthy
    To touch her virgin hand.

Rev. Hugh F. Blunt

THE ADVOCATE OF HOPELESS CASES

St. Peter holds the keys of Heaven's gate,
Kind, but severe he is, old legends state;
For the poorest comer he finds a place,
If he lived and died in the Lord's sweet grace.
But if anyone comes who spent his days
Far from God and His blessed ways,
Neither crown nor sceptre could favor win,
Nor the Pope himself might enter in.

Who knocks so? — 'Tis a mighty lord.
Was his life a good one to record?
Did he keep God's precepts night and day? —
No. — No Heaven for him. Away! away! —
And who is this other? — A miser. — Go!
No lover of money will Jesus know. —
And the third? — A clever attorney. — Nay,
No conscienceless lawyer admit I may. —
This other one! What hath he to show?
Some eloquent writings. Let him go.
And this artist? — Great things hath he done. —
Here by good works alone is glory won. —
Ha! this valiant soldier! how died he? —
He fought, lest his honor should tarnish'd be,
And so was slain. — But Our Lord once said,
When He to Caiphas' hall was led,

LEGENDS OF ST. JOSEPH 195

And cruelly struck, as the Scriptures say:
"From him who strikes turn not away." —
Now, who is this lady, in robes so fine? —
On earth, her beauty was call'd divine.
So ample her robes, it took folding-doors,
To open her way to her marble floors. —
Ah! narrow the way is Our Lord hath made;
The broad way she chose, I am sore afraid.
The flowery path leads down to hell,
The thorny to Heaven, as sages tell.
If Heaven were gain'd by the easy way,
What need were there, then, to fast and pray?
The just would have vigils and tears in vain,
And sinners the profit, without the pain.

In Naples, a story like this is told,
A simple tale of the ages old,
From which may be taken both bad and good,
According to what is the hearer's mood.
By people in health it is oft abused,
And by the dying with profit used.
'Mongst the Lazzaroni it, then, occurr'd.
And the tale full many a heart hath stirr'd.

Since Peter first kept watch and ward,
A moment he had not been off guard;
Yet sinners so many had found their way
Into Heaven, he knew not what to say.
"If those people are happy now", said he,
" 'Tis not my fault, as all may see;
For, as to me, I take good care
That no such persons shall enter there."
The beloved Apostle went that way:
"What aileth thee, Peter?" he stopped to say.

"Is anything wrong with the Church below?" —
"No, I fear for the Church up here." — "How so?"
"Say, hast thou not mark'd some faces here
That little fitted for Heaven appear?
They needs must have led bad lives below;
You have but to look at them to know
That Heaven has cost them less to buy,
Ay, an hundred-fold, than you or I."
—"'Tis true", said John, "but you're not to blame;
The keys of Heaven you kept the same."
"I know", said Peter, "but now, you see,
'Tis Joseph makes all this trouble for me.
Let people on earth be what they may,
Though they spend their lives in the very worst way,
If they call upon him when death draws near,
And cry '*Mea culpa*', he brings them here.
How he gets them in, why, I cannot tell;
But 'tis not by my gate, I know full well.
Now, John, we must let the Master know."
—"You may try", said John, "but before you go,
I tell you that Peter has but small chance
Should Joseph to plead his cause advance."
Then Peter bethought him 'twere well to take
Advice, and of John a guide to make.
"Dear Apostle", said he, "I remember now
How the Lord loved him of the gentle brow:
When at the supper He told us all
'Into treachery one of you twelve shall fall',
I, like the others, was stupified,
And dared not ask 'How shall this woe betide?'
How you on the Master's bosom lay,
And were not afraid such words to say.

So then I made you a sign to speak,
And He turn'd to you with aspect meek,
When we all shrank from His searching eye,
And, of all, was none more afraid than I.
Now, come with me, John, and I will not fear."
— Together they seek the Master dear;
Peter looking a little confused,
And John, as though he were much amused.
Full soon they saw the Savior stand
With Mary and Joseph on either hand.
"What would'st thou, Peter?" the Master said.
"I am troubled, dear Lord", and he rais'd his head.
"John will tell Thee why I grieve,—
It is that, without let or leave,
All sorts of people Joseph lets in,
Even those who have spent their life in sin;
If, at their death on him they call,
Why, into Heaven he brings them all;—
Indeed, good Lord, it is hardly fair
To those who serve Thee well down there."
—"But, Peter, if I forgive his sins,
A heavenly crown the sinner wins,—
No soul to Heaven hath Joseph brought
Who had not first My mercy sought."
—"I know", said Peter, "to die in grace
Is all that is needed to see Thy Face;
'Twas thus the good thief got entrance here,
And such cases there may be yet, that's clear,—
But, methinks 'tis not well for the Church below,
That these elect of Joseph's to Heaven go:
If people on earth should come to hear
That such sinners may find an entrance here,

My successors may thunder forth in vain
The terrible judgments, the endless pain,
Awaiting the sinner beyond the grave
Who, in life, seeketh not his soul to save."
— "Peter, 'tis true; but yet, I pray,
How could I say My Father nay?
For Thee, friend Peter, let none in
Who cannot show pardon for their sin."
—"But if Joseph goes on in this singular way,
What use is in my keeping watch, I say?
I close the gate, but the walls they scale,
I'm sorry to have to tell the tale."

FAVORS TO DEVOTED CLIENTS

A Miraculous Staircase

In Santa Fe, New Mexico, may be seen Our Lady of Light Chapel, in charge of the Sisters of Loreto. During the course of its construction (1873-1878), a difficulty arose over the erection of a staircase to the very high choir loft. Therefore, that part of the edifice was left unfinished for several years until an unknown carpenter came to the convent, seeking employment. The Sisters showed him their choir loft and the limited space available to erect a staircase. He assured them he would be able to build one, and so they let him undertake the task.

He built the beautiful wooden spiral staircase that may be seen today by visitors to Santa Fe. Each section is perfectly fitted in a groove, — not a nail being used in its construction. Architects from all sections of the country go to inspect this unique and marvelous piece of craftsmanship.

When the work was completed and the Sister Superior of the convent wished to pay the man for his service, he was nowhere to be found. According to legend, the unknown carpenter was none other than St. Joseph, in whose honor the Sisters had communicated every Wednesday that he might assist them in erecting a staircase.

* * *

St. Joseph is the patron and protector of all the Homes of the Little Sisters of the Poor, in which God's aged poor are tenderly guarded and served. Their confidence that he ever watches over the needs of their charges will appear from the following extracts from their daily experiences:

During the lifetime of their foundress, Jeanne Jugan, at the Home of the Holy Trinity in Angers, France, there was no more butter to spread on the old women's crusts, or that of the Little Sisters. In the evening on her return from collecting, Jeanne was greeted with lamentations by the Sister in charge of the Refectory. "What!" she cried, "there's no more butter, and you haven't asked St. Joseph for any?" Then she went into the little room which was used as a parlor, arranged the empty butter-dishes in the center of the table, placed one of them upside down and, with due respect, placed on this improvised pedestal a statuette of the Holy Patriarch. But would their visitors understand? "Write", said Jeanne to the **Refectoiriere**, presenting her with a wide strip of paper, "write in large capitals: 'Kind St. Joseph, send us some butter for our poor old women'."

The inscription was placed before the statuette and a votive light left burning at its feet. Then the Sisters waited to see what the effects on their visitors would be, and if, in the words of the chronicle, some people were amused at what they called "this childish confidence", others were moved to generosity. One of the Sisters recorded that "a few days later a large quantity of butter was brought to the Home; no one ever knew by whom".

* * *

In the sewing room in the Home of St. Joseph, conducted by the Little Sisters of the Poor on West 106th Street, New York City, there was a cabinet in which the old ladies stored patterns and materials. One day a certain Mary, after ironing, placed the hot electrical device on top of the cabinet, neglecting to pull out the plug. She left the room for the night.

The following morning the Little Sister while making her round discovered that St. Joseph had saved the house from fire. The iron had burned through the cabinet and fallen inside, burning the contents until it reached a picture of St. Joseph. The picture was unharmed, and everything beneath it was safe. All thanks to St. Joseph!

* * *

The courtyard of the same house of the Little Sisters was in very bad condition. Plans had been made to fill it in, pave it, and fix up the Shrines, but the money necessary for the work was lacking. The Sisters and the old people commenced a novena to St. Joseph, and put a check for the amount needed at the base of his statue. Not long after, a generous benefactor sent a check for more than was necessary to complete the work. St. Joseph never fails!

* * *

In St. John's Home, conducted by the Little Sisters of the Poor in Evansville, Indiana, the Good Mother desired to surprise all the old people with a large candy Easter egg. However, the cost prohibited her from spending so large a sum on something that really wasn't a necessity. The Sisters petitioned St. Joseph to come to their aid, which he did on Holy Saturday evening. The door bell rang. A merchant from the neighborhood had sent a large tray of chocolate Easter eggs, sufficient to care for each of their aged guests.

* * *

At their Home on East 70th Street, New York City, the Sisters needed a new altar for their chapel, as the one in use was over seventy-five years old and was commencing to fall apart. They told St. Joseph of their need, and the old people started to pray. The begging Sisters set out to find a benefactor, and in a very short time they met a kindly disposed person who was willing to give the new altar. He had it constructed to their requirements, though this necessitated an outlay of $1,500.00

St. Joseph had rewarded the confidence of his clients.

* * *

In this same house an elevator was needed to enable the Sisters to serve hot meals to their dear old guests and to transport the infirm from one floor to another. As usual, St. Joseph was petitioned, and good St. Joseph inspired a generous benefactor to install the elevator.

* * *

During the coal shortage several years ago, before the Sisters began to use oil for heating purposes, their coal supply was dangerously close to exhaustion. The aged man, in charge of the furnace room, told the Good Mother not to worry, as St. Joseph would provide. With the few pennies he called his own he went forth and purchased four paper roses; returning, he fashioned two vases out of tin cans and placed them with his precious flowers at the foot of St. Joseph's statue in the cellar. Every day he invited several of the old men to his domain to pray with him that the small pile of coal would suffice for their needs. And, behold, the small supply never diminished; it lasted through the emergency. Thanks to St. Joseph and the confident prayers of the old men!

* * *

At Brooklyn (St. Augustine), the Little Sisters

on night duty, coming back from a sick-call, heard a noise of running water; they went to look and found a leak in a pipe. They turned off the main, and while they were waiting for the plumber one of the Little Sisters accidentally dropped a small statue of St. Joseph into the space between the elevator and the floor. In order to recover it she asked a workman to open the door securing the cage of the elevator in the basement. As soon as he did so, there was a rush of water, a large quantity having accumulated there on account of the leak, without being noticed!

Although the workman was not a Catholic he saw the hand of Providence here, and observed that there might have been a serious accident, since the water had almost reached the motor which worked the elevator. As he handed the statuette to the Little Sister, he said: "You see, it was St. Joseph who let you know that there was danger here, and that's why he let himself fall so that we had to go looking for him".

* * *

In one of their Homes St. Joseph had obtained for them a good shoemaker, who rendered great service for two years. Unfortunately he knew nothing about the Catholic religion; he was not even baptized. Having fallen seriously ill, he was put in the infirmary. Near his bed was a picture representing the death of St. Joseph. The Little Sister said to him: "Look at this picture; would you not like to die in the same manner as St. Joseph?" "Who was St. Joseph?" he asked.

The Little Sister related to him the life of the foster-father of Jesus; then she explained the mysteries of the Incarnation and Redemption. The sick man listened intently; the hour of grace was striking for him. "Go and ask the Priest to come and speak to me", he said. He was baptized at the age of seventy-four; made his first Holy Communion, and, thanks to St. Joseph, had a death that might well be desired.

* * *

An old man, a non-Catholic, ninety-nine years of age, went willingly to the chapel in one of the Homes of the Little Sisters, without showing any desire of conversion. He was a great reader, and liked very much to look at a picture of the Holy Family, in which St. Joseph was represented in his workshop. "That is my Saint", he said. "I like him because he works." However, on account of his advanced age, he was soon obliged to stay in bed and he began to think of his soul.

He had been placed in the Home by the Bishop. One day he said to the Little Sister in the infirmary: "Ask Good Mother to get the Bishop to come and see me. I want to speak to him". His

Lordship came without delay. The old man was very happy when he came, and said: "I am going to die very soon, and I want to become a Catholic. Knowing that you could give me all the Sacraments at once, I asked for you to give a pleasant surprise to my Little Sisters. I want to be called Joseph". A short time later he died a child of the Catholic Church, in the act of blessing God.

* * *

The following is an incident which took place in 1871 in the Home of the Little Sisters in Dinan, France:

Each morning the old people's coffee was sweetened with treacle. The barrel being nearly empty Good Mother wrote to the usual provision merchant at Nantes, asking him to send another. He hastened to reply that he would send it at the usual price, but that he could not guarantee to deliver it. This alarmed Good Mother, who made inquiries amongst the provision merchants at Dinan, but alas! the high price would not permit her to make the purchase.

In the meantime the Little Sister in charge of the kitchen came to tell her: "The barrel of treacle is empty; there is no more for breakfast". Good Mother replied: "You must settle with St. Joseph. I have not been able to get any".

Full of confidence, the Little Sister put a medal

of St. Joseph into the barrel, and immediately the treacle began to flow; the same thing happened the next morning. They looked into the barrel and found it empty; they plunged in a stick but there was no sign of treacle. At that time there were several strangers in the Home who had taken refuge with the Sisters on account of the war. They also wished to verify this wonderful occurrence: the barrel was empty, and yet when the treacle was needed it began to flow, not abundantly, but only a little at a time, and just enough for breakfast. This lasted for a week, when, to Good Mother's great surprise, there arrived at the Home a barrel of treacle, sent by the merchant at Nantes; which was very extraordinary because, as a rule, the Little Sisters were obliged to go to the railway station and bring it to the Home themselves.

From that moment the treacle ceased to flow. Divine Providence had no longer need to manifest its protection in a miraculous way.

* * *

Eighteen years later a similar incident took place at Dublin, though under different circumstances. This time it was the meat which failed. The Little Sister in the kitchen was in great distress. On Thursday she had emptied the last barrel of salt meat, which was her usual resource. She placed St. Joseph's statue on the barrel and began a novena. The following Tuesday evening the doorbell rang loudly; a railway delivery van had stopped before the house. "Give me a hand," said the driver, "for I have a load of more than 109 pounds of meat." After the first moment of surprise the Little Sister asked him who had sent it. "I know nothing about that, Sister," he replied, "but would you please sign my paper."

The sender's name was not on the receipt, only the name of the place where it came from, and the Sisters knew of no one in that neighborhood. Tears of joy stood in the eyes of the Sisters when they saw they had received nearly the half of a large ox. Surely it was the answer from St. Joseph!

* * *

At their Home of The Holy Rosary in Santiago, Chili, the cows were very old and did not give enough milk for their needs. For several months St. Joseph had been invoked without any apparent success. The Little Sister who dispensed the milk asked for another fervent novena. In order to attract the attention of their holy Protector to her request, she placed at the feet of his statue the picture of a Dutch cow, cut out of a catalogue, confiding to St. Joseph her great desire to have a similar one.

The following day she asked permission to explain the object of her novena to the begging Sisters, who promised to do their best to find the animal, knowing it was superior to the ordinary cows of the country. They set out, uncertain as to which door they should direct their steps. But St. Joseph does not need an introduction. "We shall commence our begging as usual", said the Little Sisters.

They had already been in several parts of the town, when a lady came up to them. "Sister, would you please pray for my husband who is not a Catholic. I, myself, am a Catholic. I have tried to convert him and he is favorably inclined, but as yet he has not reached a decision." Saying this, she slipped an offering into the Sister's hand. They thanked her, and promised to recommend her intention to the united prayers of the Community and the old people. "Trust in God, Madam; you are sure to obtain it. We are also asking something from St. Joseph, and we are sure he will give it to us. We want a good cow; those we have are no longer sufficient for the needs of the Home; there are so many poor." "Ah!" said the lady, "a cow — my husband has some; I am sure he would willingly give you one. Today he has gone to our country house. Come and have lunch with me and afterwards we could motor down to him."

"Thank you very much, Madam, but we cannot accept your kind invitation. Good Mother would be anxious; she is expecting us home." "Very well, go home and tell her, and come back at half past one." The begging Sisters did not need to be told twice. Everything was settled, and at four o'clock they reached the country house. The gentleman heard the motor and was waiting for them. Madam was the first to alight, and said: "I have brought the Little Sisters to see you; they want a cow". "Yes ours are so old; they scarcely give any milk." "They have such a lot of old people", Madam added kindly. Deep in thought, no doubt seeking which one he would give, her husband replied benevolently, "It is quite easy".

"If you do not mind, we should like to have a Dutch cow", said the Little Sister, as if to help him in making a choice.

"A Dutch cow! Oh, Sister! that would deprive me of too much. I have only one; I gave five hundred francs for her, and it was so difficult to have her brought out here."

"The Little Sister who wants the cow is from Holland." Sister replied. "Ah, that's why, she knows the good qualities of that particular breed." "Yes! she has put the picture of one at St. Joseph's feet; she is sure to get it."

"Who is St. Joseph?" asked the non-Catholic, at the same time making a sign to a servant to approach. The Little Sister had already the small statue of St. Joseph in her hand, and in a few words she explained the role of their holy Protector in their Homes. She spoke of the begging, of the poor old people whom they receive, of the happiness which they procure for them on earth, with a view of leading them gently on the way to Heaven.

Visibly touched, the gentleman said: "Will you give me the little statue? Tomorrow afternoon you will have the Dutch cow".

What joy not only for the begging Sisters and the whole Community, but also for the kind lady! However, the story is not yet finished. Within a month, grace was besieging their gracious benefactor, who had been St. Joseph's assistant. At last he yielded; his renouncement of his former beliefs and baptism as a Catholic rendered his wife and himself completely happy. Once more St. Joseph had heard the trusting prayers of his devoted clients!

* * *

The following event took place at the Home of the new foundation of the Home of the Little Sisters at San Francisco in 1903. Foreseeing the great quantity of water that would be necessary for the Home, they decided to dig a well. After a first fruitless attempt, at a depth of eighty feet they came to rock. The contractor said: "The stream is lower down in the valley". He was advised to try a little further away; "St. Joseph must find the water for us". The workmen began again; once more they arrived at a depth of eighty feet without any sign of water. They wanted to stop, but the old people entreated them to continue digging, saying: "St. Joseph is sure to find water for us". They prayed very fervently; a candle was burning before his statue, and they promised to recite the "Miserere" for three days. The Little Sisters offered their sacrifices for the same intention. Then they threw some holy water and a medal of St. Joseph into the shaft, advising the workmen: "Now, dig; go deeper. This time it is sure; St. Joseph will give the water to us".

Praise be to St. Joseph! At a depth of a hundred and twenty feet a source sprang up, which yielded three thousand gallons an hour. The gratitude of the Sisters and the old people's joy can be better imagined than described. Candles were lit in the chapel, and the "Te Deum" was sung in thanksgiving.

* * *

It was a very severe winter in England; snow had been falling for several days, so that it was impossible for the Sisters' van to go out. The bread was short; there was not enough for the supper and no hope of getting any. About two o'clock in the afternoon Good Mother sent out the begging Sisters, on foot, saying: "Ask St. Joseph to find at least enough bread for supper". Then she went to the rooms and asked the old people to pray for this intention.

The Sisters had been walking for some time when they met a gentleman, who asked them where they were going in such awful weather. They replied: "There is no more bread in the house; we are going to look for some for our old people". "You may go home again", he said. "I own a bakery. This morning my workmen made too much bread and, on account of the bad weather, I have not been able to sell it. I shall send it to you." An hour later five men from the bakery brought the bread to the Home.

The old people began to pray once more, but this time it was in thanksgiving.

* * *

On the eve of the Epiphany, at Madrid (St. Louis), the Little Sisters, during recreation, were singing a hymn to St. Joseph asking him to send a surprise for the old people. Whilst they were singing the bell rang: some benefactors had brought a number of small boxes of nougat for their poor, who declared that the Three Kings had never before given them such a treat.

* * *

As it was nightfall before the Little Sisters returned from their questing, having been delayed by their van breaking down, they were anxious to reach a neighboring village as soon as possible, where they would be sure of being given hospitality. But the chauffeur did not know the way, and was moving along very slowly.

They turned to St. Joseph for help, and at that very moment a passerby jumped on to the running-board, and asked: "Would you be so good as to give me a lift as far as X?" "Certainly, we are going there too. But could you tell us the shortest way?"

"Turn to the left and go straight ahead."

When they reached the village the unknown traveller said to the chauffeur: "Here we are, thank you very much". And jumping off, he disappeared.

* * *

Every evening the Sisters in Messina pay a visit to the statue of St. Joseph at their front door and sing the "Memorare". On one occasion he was holding in his hand a picture of a typewriter. The Sisters already had the machine, but it was not quite paid for, though some benefactors had promised to give something towards it each month. As the Sisters had been asked to finish paying for it, they told St. Joseph: "Send us, please, the money to pay this debt, and we will take the picture away". A telephone call from the wife of the Chief Commissioner of Police informed them that her husband had been given a large alms for them. This news was confirmed by one of the staff, who told the Sisters that the gift was intended to cover the cost of a typewriter!

* * *

One Wednesday — St. Joseph's day — a stranger handed in at the front door of the Home of the Little Sisters in Plymouth, England, a small and carefully secured parcel, saying: "Would you be so good as to give this to the person in charge of this house".

The Good Mother, who had been praying to St. Joseph to send her some money, opened the package and found to her surprise and delight a bundle of notes with these lines: "I have always wanted to give some tangible proof of the good that you do, and that is why I am sending you this money, knowing that you will make good use of it!"

* * *

The hot water from the kitchen stove suddenly refused to flow in their Home in Granada, Spain. The workman, having spent considerable time examining the system without being able to discover the difficulty, wanted to dismantle the stove. The Good Mother objected strongly. "We will let St. Joseph take care of this", she said: "Come back tomorrow and we shall see."

Next morning the water came out with full force as soon as the taps were turned on. Imagine the astonishment of the plumbers and the gratitude of the Little Sisters! During the night St. Joseph had changed his occupation of carpenter for that of a plumber!

* * *

In one of their Homes in the south, the balconies are provided with blinds to protect the old people from the heat of the sun in summer time. The material from which they were made was worn out and had been patched so often that it seemed impossible to do anything more with them.

The Good Mother was hoping to replace them, but found herself quite unable to afford the expense, and when the old ladies tried without success to repair the blinds one of them suggested asking St. Joseph to take the matter in hand.

A novena was begun, and on the third day a young stranger made his appearance. He had heard about the work of the Sisters and was anxious to make a contribution. He offered some vegetables from his garden, and inquired about their needs. He was told about the lamentable state of the blinds; the matter interested him, and a couple of hours later he returned with patterns and a manufacturer of blinds. The measurements were taken and the order given, but the manufacturer had no more idea than the Sisters of the identity of the generous donor, who had paid in advance for the blinds. "This", he said, "is one of those things that happen only once in a lifetime!"

As for the Sisters, they bless St. Joseph's messenger, who said when he was leaving them: "Pray that I may be admitted to the Trappist monastery". They have never seen him since.

* * *

On the eve of the Feast of St. Joseph last year in Marseilles the Little Sisters had not a flower for his altar. So the Good Mother sent the questing Sisters to the flower market, but everything was so dear! Timidly they approached the flower sellers who were raffling a large chocolate Easter egg. Impossible to disturb them at this occupation, they thought.

But lo! One of them recognized the black cloaks, and said: "Come here, Little Sisters, come and draw the winning number!" Without hesitation they agreed, and they even presented to the winner the beautiful Easter egg. She in her excitement asked: "What can I give you in return?"

"If you please, Madam, some flowers for St. Joseph; we have none for his altar."

"Oh, if that's all you want, take the lot, he certainly deserves them!"

Lilies and beautiful pinks passed from the florist's stand to the Little Sisters' van. They returned in triumph, saying: "Thank you, St. Joseph. You have blessed our obedience!"

The Feast was kept with gladness and thanksgiving. But during the following week complaints were heard in the old men's infirmary: "In the room below they have a wireless set, and we, nothing!" True; but since even a small wireless is too expensive, the Good Mother promised to pray to St. Joseph.

Immediately a novena was begun. On the third day an officer called. "Good Mother", he said, "we have installed a large wireless set for the soldiers in the barracks, and the colonel wanted to know what was to be done with the old set which is still in good condition. The soldiers all answered: 'Give it to the Little Sisters of the Poor for the old people!... Won't you?'"

Learning that the old men were praying to St. Joseph for one, the officer was overjoyed, and said: "So, I am St. Joseph! How glad I am to be able to give pleasure to the old fellows, all the more so since I knew nothing about it".

The wireless was fixed up at once and tuned in: the old men wept for joy when they heard "St. Joseph's radio!"

* * *

The experience of the Sisters has been that whatever favor is desired is granted according to the way it is asked. For instance, (1) in one of their Homes in Europe during the second World War the old men had nothing to smoke. One of the Sisters on her routine tour of begging found a wet cigar on the street and brought it home. It was placed at the feet of St. Joseph's statue, and he was told that they were in need of some cigars. In a few days an army truck drove up and presented boxes of "wet" cigars.

(2) Another time, potatoes were needed. The Sisters had only a sprouting potato. This was placed at the feet of St. Joseph's statue, with the request that he obtain potatoes. In a day or two a farmer brought a number of sacks of potatoes "sprouting".

(3) In one of their Homes they were in great need of a man to help the Sisters in the kitchen. They clipped from a newspaper the picture of a nice old man, and placed it at the feet of St. Joseph. They had not noticed that in cutting out the picture they cut off one arm. A few days later a destitute old man, with but one arm, came and asked to be taken into the Home, stating that he would like to help the Sisters with their work. He was assigned to the kitchen, and rendered many services.

(4) In one of their Brooklyn Homes the old men had no beer to drink for some time, so the old men placed their empty cans in front of St. Joseph's statue to remind him of their need. A Priest

visiting the Home passed the statue and asked the Good Mother what the beer cans were doing there in front of the statue. She told him that the old men were asking St. Joseph for beer. On his way back to his rectory on the subway the Priest was enjoying a private chuckle over the story, when a stranger who sat opposite came over and asked to share the joke. The Priest told him the story, and the stranger announced that as Vice-President of a large beer company he would see that the old men would never want for beer again as long as he lived. Within a few days a large delivery of beer was made to the Home of the Little Sisters of the Poor with the stranger's compliments.

* * *

The devotion of the Little Sisters to St. Joseph is well known, but, naturally, it is not generally known that each Sister is allowed to have among her few personal possessions a tiny statue of St. Joseph with the Child Jesus in his arms. In all probability this custom goes back to the very early days of the Congregation, since the little statue possessed by the Foundress herself has its story. It happened at the time when the London house, Portobello Road, was being enlarged. There was practically no money in hand. Still that did not deter Good Mother Agnes-Onesime, and the work was commenced.

One day the Good Mother was visited by a lady whose daughter had years before received a statuette from Jeanne Jugan herself at Saint-Servan. The daughter had given it to her mother, and so great was her admiration for the newly established and rapidly spreading work of the Little Sisters and for the saintliness of the Foundress, that she took most jealous care of the statuette and looked upon it as a sort of relic. She had it fitted into an elegant little case, which she wore on the end of her watch chain. Now that her daughter had entered the novitiate of the nuns of the Sacred Heart, she decided to give the little statue to Jeanne Jugan's daughters.

The Good Mother was immersed in the worries of the building operations, and she placed the statuette alongside the money that had been begged. Now the amazing thing was that on several occasions when she opened her cash box she found more money in it than she had placed therein. She related the fact several times to the Mother Provincial. This multiplication of the funds was attributed to St. Joseph, and he was implored to continue the good work until the building was finished. This particular statue is now in the museum at the motherhouse.

Each Little Sister always carries a similar statuette with her; her thoughts turn to it in every conceivable difficulty. It will be held in her hand when she stands in need of strength and inspiration. St. Joseph has never failed her yet!

* * *

In 1906 an earthquake had completely destroyed the Little Sisters' Home at Valparaiso, Chili. Eight of the Sisters and several of the old people were victims of the disaster. The survivors had taken refuge in the two Homes at Santiago, but naturally they wished to return to Valparaiso. When reconstruction commenced in the ruined area the Little Sisters thought they, too, should try to re-erect their house. But how could they attempt it?

Their thoughts turned to one of the benefactresses of the first Home, who had been very good to them. This great lady, however, did not like to be asked, preferring to distribute her gifts as she pleased. Good Mother Clarisse was well aware of this and trembled at the very thought of an interview. To give herself courage she held hidden in one hand the statuette of St. Joseph. Unfortunately, the timid request was clearly inopportune; the interview regarding the proposed construction was terminated, and there remained nothing but for her to withdraw. The Good Mother was apologizing for the intrusion, when out of her trembling hand fell the little statue.... Quickly she stooped down to pick it up, but both the action and the object aroused the curiosity of the benefactress. There was nothing to do but to explain that St. Joseph had been thus pressed into service in order to plead the cause of the poor. That was sufficient; the lady experienced a sudden change in her attitude, and said: "It shall be as you require. St. Joseph has victoriously pleaded their cause. I am now going to see what we can do to provide them with a large house as soon as possible".

Eighteen months later the Home of Vina del Mar replaced that of Valparaiso and opened its doors to those who had escaped the earthquake.

* * *

The statuette has also played a great part in the thorny difficulties involved in the acquisition of property and new foundations. Time and again the Little Sisters have left the statuette in the grounds, or have thrown it over the walls, and the great Carpenter has taken clandestine possession of coveted property before any signing of contracts, even before the proprietor has had the slightest intention of selling. When the good Saint is compromised in this fashion by the confidence of the Little Sisters and installed where they want to go with their old people, victory is pretty well certain. In all confidence they say, "St. Joseph is there.... We shall soon be there too".

Sometimes the little statue also performs its

marvels quite openly. A meadow adjoining a house which had been opened the year before was indispensable for its development. When the Mother Provincial asked the proprietor to sell it, she met with a categoric refusal. He was offered a statuette, with the secret hope that it might help him to change his mind. Two days later — a Wednesday — the proprietor came himself and offered the meadow **for nothing!**

* * *

The devotion to St. Joseph by the Little Sisters of the Poor is that of almost all Religious Orders, and could be continued indefinitely. Hundreds of convents and monasteries have been named in honor of this great Saint. Many Religious Communities have been consecrated to him as their special exemplar and protector. Suffice it to mention just one of them — the Sisters of St. Joseph.

In 1856 three Sisters of St. Joseph came to Brooklyn, New York, from the Philadelphia, Pennsylvania, motherhouse to open a school in the Diocese of Brooklyn. Today, under the patronage of St. Joseph, the Congregation has grown to 1,700 Sisters, with 70 schools and 2 hospitals in its care. Throughout its entire history the Congregation has been conscious of the sustained protection of St. Joseph, and all their works are under his patronage.

The Sisters have as their ideal to imitate the care and solicitude shown by St. Joseph to his foster-Son and his Immaculate Spouse. In their work of education they look to him as "the most excellent educator of our Lord Jesus Christ". Before each class period the blessing of St. Joseph is envoked: "All for Jesus, Mary and Joseph". In every school conducted by the Sisters of St. Joseph his statue stands in a prominent place, and it is pointed out to visitors under the title, "Prefect of Discipline". He has shown his loving care and watchfulness over the Congregation for almost one hundred years.

Among the many instances which show the special protection of St. Joseph are the following:

Sister St. Joseph, from the Flushing, New York, motherhouse, was traveling from Webster, Mass., to Brattleboro, Vt., in a heavy snow storm. At a lonely depot she found herself stranded late at night, with no train due for several hours. She prayed to St. Joseph for help, and soon she was approached by a venerable white-bearded gentleman, who offered to take her to the parish house. Sister St. Joseph followed him into his sleigh, feeling a strange confidence. Soon arriving at the local rectory she told the parish Priest of the stranger who had conducted her, but when she looked for the old gentleman to thank him he was not to be found. The

Community has always felt that St. Joseph himself had been the guide of the Sister in her plight.

* * *

Through the application of oil from candles burned at the shrine of St. Joseph in the motherhouse at Brentwood, New York, and the prayers of the Sisters of St. Joseph, a small child who wore a brace was cured. The brace, which the child discarded, was then left before the shrine of St. Joseph, where it could be seen for many years.

PART V

THE LITTLE OFFICE OF ST. JOSEPH

Hail, glory of the Patriarchs, steward of God's holy Church, who didst preserve the Bread of Life and the Wheat of the Elect.

Versicle. Thou, O Lord, wilt open my lips.

Responsory. And my mouth shall announce Thy praise.

V. Incline unto my aid, O God!

R. O Lord, make haste to help me.

V. Glory be to the Father, and to the Son, and to the Holy Ghost,

R. As it was in the beginning, is now, and ever shall be, world without end. Amen.

HYMN

Mighty Joseph, son of David!
  High and glorious in thy state —
Of Our Lord the foster-father,
  Mary's spouse immaculate.
The Almighty's faithful servant,
  Of the Holy Family
Head and father. Oh! I pray thee
  Be a father unto me.

Antiphon. He made him master of His house, and ruler over all His possessions. (Psalm 104: 21.)

V. Pray for us, most blessed Joseph,

R. That we may be made worthy of the promises of Christ.

Let us Pray.

May we, O Lord, we beseech Thee, be assisted by the merits of the spouse of Thy most holy Mother, that what of ourselves we cannot possibly obtain, may through his intercession be granted to us by Thee, Who livest and reignest God forever and ever. Amen.

V. O Lord, hear my prayer,
R. And let my cry come unto Thee.
V. Let us bless the Lord.
R. Thanks be to God.
V. May the souls of the faithful departed through the mercy of God rest in peace.
R. Amen.

PRIME

Hail, glory of the Patriarchs, steward of God's holy Church, who didst preserve the Bread of Life and the Wheat of the Elect.

V. Thou, O Lord, wilt open my lips,
R. And my mouth shall announce Thy praise.
V. Incline unto my aid, O God!
R. O Lord, make haste to help me.
V. Glory be to the Father, and to the Son, and to the Holy Ghost,
R. As it was in the beginning, is now, and ever shall be, world without end. Amen.

HYMN

Sorely was thy bosom troubled
    Till the mystery was revealed
Which the Lord had wrought in Mary,
    Who in patience all concealed.

But an angel soon from heaven
> Bids thy loving doubts to cease:
So may every care and trial
> Turn for me to joy and peace.

Antiphon. Joseph, son of David, fear not to take unto thee Mary thy spouse, for what is conceived in her is of the Holy Ghost.

V. Pray for us, most blessed Joseph.

R. That we may be made worthy of the promises of Christ.

Let us Pray.

May we, O Lord, we beseech Thee, be assisted by the merits of the spouse of Thy most holy Mother, that what of ourselves we cannot possibly obtain, may through his intercession be granted to us by Thee, Who livest and reignest God forever and ever. Amen.

V. O Lord, hear my prayer.

R. And let my cry come unto Thee.

V. Let us bless the Lord.

R. Thanks be to God.

V. May the souls of the faithful departed through the mercy of God rest in peace.

R. Amen.

TIERCE

Hail, glory of the Patriarchs, steward of God's holy Church, who didst preserve the Bread of Life and the Wheat of the Elect.

V. Thou, O Lord, wilt open my lips,

R. And my mouth shall announce Thy praise.

V. Incline unto my aid, O God!

R. O Lord, make haste to help me.

V. Glory be to the Father, and to the Son, and to the Holy Ghost,

R. As it was in the beginning, is now, and ever shall be, world without end. Amen.

HYMN

With the Virgin, young and tender,
    In the winter-time forlorn,
Thou to Bethlehem didst journey,
    That Our Lord might there be born.

As thy God thou didst adore Him,
    While He in the manger lay,
Now is He in heaven exalted —
    Turn to Him for us and pray!

Antiphon. Joseph went up out of Galilee from Nazareth into Judea, to the city of David, which is called Bethlehem, with Mary his espoused wife, who was with child.

V. Pray for us, most blessed Joseph.

R. That we may be made worthy of the promises of Christ.

Let us Pray.

May we, O Lord, we beseech Thee, be assisted by the merits of the spouse of Thy most holy Mother, that what of ourselves we cannot possibly obtain, may through his intercession be granted to us by Thee, Who livest and reignest God forever and ever. Amen.

V. O Lord, hear my prayer.

R. And let my cry come unto Thee.

V. Let us bless the Lord.

R. Thanks be to God.

V. May the souls of the faithful departed through the mercy of God rest in peace.

R. Amen.

SEXT

Hail, glory of the Patriarchs, steward of God's holy Church, who didst preserve the Bread of Life and the Wheat of the Elect.

V. Thou, O Lord, wilt open my lips,

R. And my mouth shall announce Thy praise.

V. Incline unto my aid, O God!

R. O Lord, make haste to help me.

V. Glory be to the Father, and to the Son, and to the Holy Ghost,

R. As it was in the beginning, is now, and ever shall be, world without end. Amen.

HYMN

Fleeing at the angel's warning,
   Far from Herod's fury wild,
Long in Egypt didst thou tarry
   With the Virgin and the Child.
By thy toil, and pain, and sadness,
   In that exile dark and drear,
Help me in the cares and sorrows
   Which may be my portion here.

Antiphon. Arise and take the Child and His Mother, and fly into Egypt, and be there until I shall tell thee; for it will come to pass that Herod will seek the Child to destroy Him. (Matt. 2: 13.)

V. Pray for us, most blessed Joseph.

R. That we may be made worthy of the promises of Christ.

Let us Pray.

May we, O Lord, we beseech Thee, be assisted by the merits of the spouse of Thy most holy Mother, that what of ourselves we cannot possibly obtain, may through his intercession be granted to us by Thee, Who livest and reignest God forever and ever. Amen.

V. O Lord, hear my prayer.

R. And let my cry come unto Thee.

V. Let us bless the Lord.

R. Thanks be to God.

V. May the souls of the faithful departed through the mercy of God rest in peace.

R. Amen.

NONE

Hail, glory of the Patriarchs, steward of God's holy Church, who didst preserve the Bread of Life and the Wheat of the Elect.

V. Thou, O Lord, wilt open my lips,

R. And my mouth shall announce Thy praise.

V. Incline unto my aid, O God!

R. O Lord, make haste to help me.

V. Glory be to the Father, and to the Son, and to the Holy Ghost,

R. As it was in the beginning, is now, and ever shall be, world without end. Amen.

HYMN

Home from Egypt's land returning
 Thou wouldst rest in Galilee,
But to Nazareth art bidden,
 That the Child secure may be.
Souls retiring, sweet and humble,
 Thou dost still for Jesus seek:
That my heart may be His garden
 Make it humble, pure and meek.

Antiphon. Who arose, and took the Child and His Mother and came into the land of Israel ... and he dwelt in a city which is called Nazareth. (Matt. 2: 23.)

V. Pray for us, most blessed Joseph.

R. That we may be made worthy of the promises of Christ.

Let us Pray.

May we, O Lord, we beseech Thee, be assisted by the merits of the spouse of Thy most holy Mother, that what of ourselves we cannot possibly obtain, may through his intercession be granted to us by Thee, Who livest and reignest God forever and ever. Amen.

V. O Lord, hear my prayer.

R. And let my cry come unto Thee.

V. Let us bless the Lord.

R. Thanks be to God.

V. May the souls of the faithful departed through the mercy of God rest in peace.

R. Amen.

VESPERS

Hail, glory of the Patriarchs, steward of God's holy Church, who didst preserve the Bread of Life and the Wheat of the Elect.

V. Thou, O Lord, wilt open my lips,

R. And my mouth shall announce Thy praise.

V. Incline unto my aid, O God!

R. O Lord, make haste to help me.

V. Glory be to the Father, and to the Son, and to the Holy Ghost,

R. As it was in the beginning, is now, and ever shall be, world without end. Amen.

PRAYERS TO ST. JOSEPH

HYMN

Thou didst search with loving anguish
    For the little Jesus lost;
But, in finding Him, what rapture,
    Purchased at that sorrow's cost!

Thee, my light, my life, my Jesus,
    May I never lose by sin!
May my heart be pure and simple,
    So that Thou may'st rest therein.

Antiphon. Son, why hast Thou done so to us? Behold, Thy father and I have sought Thee sorrowing. (Luke 2: 48.)

V. Pray for us, most blessed Joseph.

R. That we may be made worthy of the promises of Christ.

Let us Pray.

May we, O Lord, we beseech Thee, be assisted by the merits of the spouse of Thy most holy Mother, that what of ourselves we cannot possibly obtain, may through his intercession be granted to us by Thee, Who livest and reignest God forever and ever. Amen.

V. O Lord, hear my prayer.

R. And let my cry come unto Thee.

V. Let us bless the Lord.

R. Thanks be to God.

V. May the souls of the faithful departed through the mercy of God rest in peace.

R. Amen.

COMPLINE

Hail, glory of the Patriarchs, steward of God's holy Church, who didst preserve the Bread of Life and the Wheat of the Elect.

V. Convert us, O Lord, our Salvation,

R. And turn Thine anger from us.

V. Incline unto my aid, O God!

R. O Lord, make haste to help me.

V. Glory be to the Father, and to the Son, and to the Holy Ghost,

R. As it was in the beginning, is now, and ever shall be, world without end. Amen.

HYMN

Jesus, Mary, hung above thee,
    On that sad, yet happy day,
When, with their fond arms around thee,
    Passed thy gentle soul away.

Oh! when death shall come to take me,
    All its terrors I'll defy,
If, with Jesus and with Mary,
    Thou, dear Joseph, will be nigh.

Antiphon. In peace in the selfsame I will sleep, and I will rest, for thou, O Lord, singularly hast settled me in hope. (Ps. 4: 9.)

V. Pray for us, most blessed Joseph.

R. That we may be made worthy of the promises of Christ.

Let us Pray.

May we, O Lord, we beseech Thee, be assisted by the merits of the spouse of Thy most holy Mother, that what of ourselves we cannot possibly obtain, may through his intercession be granted to us by Thee, Who livest and reignest God forever and ever. Amen.

V. O Lord, hear my prayer.

R. And let my cry come unto Thee.

V. Let us bless the Lord.

R. Thanks be to God.

V. May the souls of the faithful departed through the mercy of God rest in peace.

R. Amen.

COMMENDATION

Thus, O glorious saint, my homage
    I, thy grateful client, pay.
Hear my prayer and smile upon me,
    Guide and guard me on my way.

May I, 'neath thy kind protection,
    Safely reach my journey's close,
And with thee in heaven's bright palace
    Through eternity repose!

A MORNING OBLATION TO ST. JOSEPH

O glorious St. Joseph, accept the offering of my whole being, which I desire to present to my beloved Jesus, through thee.

Purify all; make all a perfect holocaust. May every respiration of my heart be a spiritual communion; every look and thought an act of divine love; every action a sweet sacrifice; every word an arrow of divine love; every step an advance towards Jesus; every visit to our Lord in the Blessed Sacrament as pleasing to God as the errands of the Angels; every thought of thee, dear Saint, an act to remind thee that I am thy child.

To thy care and keeping I confide the occasions on which I usually fail, particularly, N.N. Accept each little action of the day, though replete with imperfection, and offer it to Jesus, Whose mercy will overlook its defects since He regards not so much the gift as the love of the giver.

St. Joseph, spouse of the ever Immaculate Virgin Mary, the Mother of God, obtain for me a pure, humble and charitable mind, and perfect resignation to the Divine Will. Be my guide, father, and model through life, that I may merit to die as thou didst in the arms of Jesus and Mary. Amen.

SPECIAL OFFERING OF THE DAY'S WORK

O blessed St. Joseph, I offer this day's work in union with thy labors in the workshop of Nazareth, begging thee to present it to the Sacred Heart of Jesus, for all Its intentions, and in reparation for so many souls who live in idleness and refuse the labor imposed by God as just penance upon all men.

St. Joseph, friend of the Sacred Heart, protect us.

PRAYER TO ST. JOSEPH

Most blessed St. Joseph, master of the hidden life and great chief of the "Apostleship of Prayer", thou hast the key of the Sacred Heart, Which found Its rest on thine and loved thee with the devotion of a child. Teach us to live, as thou didst live, a life of prayer, to love God's Will, and to value the things of time as we shall value them in eternity.

Vouchsafe, O holy Joseph, to be mindful of us and to intercede for us with Him Who once called thee father; direct us in the path of life, and assist us, with Mary and the Angels, at the hour of our death. Amen.

St. Joseph, friend of the Sacred Heart, pray for us.

PRAYER TO ST. JOSEPH BEFORE HOLY COMMUNION

O Blessed Joseph, how sweet and wonderful a privilege was thine, not only to see, but to carry in thy arms, to kiss and to embrace with fatherly affection that only-begotten Son of God, Whom so many kings and prophets desired to see, but were not able. O! that, inspired by thy example and aided by thy patronage, I may with like feelings of love and reverence, embrace my Lord and Redeemer in the Blessed Sacrament of the Altar, so that when my life on earth is ended I may merit to embrace Him eternally in Heaven. Amen.

PRAYER TO ST. JOSEPH FOR LIGHT IN THE CHOICE OF A STATE OF LIFE

O great St. Joseph, who wert so docile to the guidance of the Holy Ghost, obtain for me the grace to know what state of life Divine Providence destines for me. Do not suffer me to be deceived with regard to so important a choice, upon which depends my happiness in this world, and even my eternal salvation. Do thou obtain for me that, being enlightened to know the Divine Will and faithful in accomplishing it, I may embrace that state of life which God has destined for me, and which will lead me to a happy eternity. Amen.

PRAYER FOR CHOICE OF A STATE OF LIFE

O my God, Thou Who art the God of Wisdom and Counsel, Thou Who readest in my heart the sincere will to please Thee alone and also to regulate my life, so far as regards the choice of a state of life conformable in everything to Thy most holy Will, grant me, through the intercession of the most blessed Virgin my Mother, and of my patron saints, especially of St. Joseph and St. Aloysius, the grace to know what state I ought to enter, and to embrace it, know it in order that I may be able to seek and promote in it Thy glory, work out my salvation, and merit that heavenly reward which Thou hast promised to those who carry out Thy divine Will. Amen.

St. Joseph, most holy guardian of Jesus and Mary, help us with thy prayers in all our necessities, both spiritual and temporal; so that we may be able with Mary and thee eternally to bless our Divine Redeemer, Jesus.

Grant us, O Lord Jesus, faithfully to imitate the examples of Thy Holy Family, so that in the hour of our death, in the company of Thy glorious Virgin Mother and St. Joseph, we may deserve to be received by Thee into eternal tabernacles.

Jesus, Mary, Joseph.

INVOCATION

O Jesus, Mary, Joseph!
    My heart is all your own;
Its hidden sweet affections
    Are ever near your throne.

My soul with all its powers,
  My life, its joy and pain,
O Jesus, Mary, Joseph!
  I give to your sweet reign.

O Jesus, Mary, Joseph!
  When shadows round me close;
When past misdeeds affright me
  Amid dark spirit foes;
When in the strong death anguish
  I gasp your names of power,
O Jesus, Mary, Joseph!
  Assist me in that hour.

O Jesus, Mary, Joseph!
  What rapture might I die
In peace, forgiven and stainless
  In your sweet company!
Your triple shield around me,
  The Trinity within,
O Jesus, Mary, Joseph!
  Heaven's glory may I win!
Marist Hymnal

SHORT DAILY ACT OF CONSECRATION TO ST. JOSEPH

O blessed Joseph, faithful guardian of my Redeemer Jesus Christ, protector of thy chaste spouse the Immaculate Virgin Mother of God, I choose thee this day to be my especial patron and advocate; and I firmly resolve to honor thee as such from this time forth and always. Therefore, I humbly beseech thee, dear St. Joseph, to receive me for thy client, to instruct me in every doubt, to comfort me in every affliction, and, finally, to defend and protect me in the hour of my death. Amen.

A DAILY PRAYER TO ST. JOSEPH

O my beloved St. Joseph! adopt me as thy child; take charge of my salvation; watch over me day and night; preserve me from occasions of sin; obtain for me purity of body and soul, and the spirit of prayer, through thy intercession with Jesus. Grant me a spirit of sacrifice, of humility, and self-denial; obtain for me a burning love for Jesus in the Blessed Sacrament, and a sweet, tender love for Mary, my Mother.

St. Joseph, be with me in life, be with me in death, and obtain for me a favorable judgment from Jesus, my merciful Savior. Amen.

St. Joseph, help us in our earthly strife,
Ever to lead a pure and blameless life.

ACT OF CONSECRATION TO ST. JOSEPH

O blessed St. Joseph! I consecrate myself to thy honor, and give myself to thee, that thou mayest always be my father, my protector, and my guide in the way of salvation. Obtain for me a great purity of heart and a fervent love of the interior life. After thy example may I do all my actions for the greater glory of God, in union with the divine Heart of Jesus and the immaculate Heart of Mary! And do thou, O blessed Joseph, pray for me, that I may experience the peace and joy of thy holy death. Amen.

MEMORARE TO ST. JOSEPH

Remember, most pure spouse of Mary ever-Virgin, my loving protector, St. Joseph, that never has it been heard that anyone ever invoked thy protection, or besought aid of thee, without being consoled. In this confidence I come before thee; I fervently recommend myself to thee. Despise not my prayer, foster-father of our Redeemer, but do thou in thy pity receive it. Amen.

FOR THOSE IN THEIR AGONY

Eternal Father, by the love which Thou bearest to St. Joseph, chosen by Thee from among all men to represent Thee on earth, have pity on us and on poor souls in their agony. Pater, Ave, Gloria.

Eternal and divine Son, by the love which Thou bearest to St. Joseph, Thy most faithful guardian on earth, have pity on us and on all poor souls in their agony. Pater, Ave, Gloria.

Eternal and divine Spirit, by the love Thou bearest to St. Joseph, who with so great solicitude watched over most holy Mary the Spouse of Thy predilection, have pity on us and on all poor souls in their agony. Pater, Ave, Gloria.

To thee, O blessed Joseph, do we fly in our tribulation, and *having implored the help of thy most holy spouse,* we confidently crave thy patronage *also*. Through that charity which bound thee to the Immaculate Virgin Mother of God, and through the paternal love with which thou didst embrace the Child Jesus, we humbly beseech thee graciously to regard the inheritance which Jesus Christ hath purchased by His Blood, and with thy power and strength to aid us in our necessities.

O most watchful Guardian of the Divine Family, defend the chosen children of Jesus Christ; O most loving Father, ward off from us every contagion of error and corrupting influence; O our most mighty protector, be propitious to us and from Heaven assist us in this our struggle with the power of darkness, and, as once thou didst rescue the Child Jesus from deadly peril, so now protect God's holy Church from the snares of the enemy and from all adversity: shield, too, each one of us by thy constant protection, so that, supported by thine example and thine aid, we may be able to live piously, to die holily, and to obtain eternal happiness in Heaven. Amen.

PRAYER TO ST. JOSEPH, PATRON OF THE UNIVERSAL CHURCH

O most powerful Patriarch, St. Joseph, Patron of that universal Church which has always invoked thee in anxieties and tribulations; from the lofty seat of thy glory lovingly regard the Catholic world. Let it move thy paternal heart to see the mystical Spouse of Christ and His Vicar weakened by sorrow and persecuted by powerful enemies. We beseech thee, by the most bitter suffering thou didst experience on earth, to wipe away in mercy the tears of the revered Pontiff, to defend and liberate him, and to intercede with the Giver of peace and charity, that every hostile power being overcome and every error being destroyed, the whole Church may serve the God of all blessings in perfect liberty: ut destructis adversitatibus et erroribus universis Ecclesia secura Deo serviat libertate. Amen.

PRAYER OF ST. BERNARDINE OF SIENA

Be mindful of us, O blessed Joseph, and intercede on our behalf with thy reputed Son; and secure for us the favor of thy most holy Virgin Spouse, the Mother of Him Who liveth and reigneth with the Father and the Holy Ghost, world without end. Amen.

O Joseph, virgin father of Jesus, most pure spouse of the Virgin Mary, pray for us daily to the Son of God, that, armed with the weapons of His grace, we may fight as we ought in life, and be crowned by Him in death.

GREAT ST. JOSEPH, SON OF DAVID

Great St. Joseph, son of David,
Foster-father of our Lord,
Spouse of Mary, ever Virgin,
Keeping o'er them watch and ward.
In the stable thou didst guard them
With a father's loving care;
Thou by God's command didst save them
From the cruel Herod's snare.

Three long days in grief and anguish,
With His Mother sweet and mild,
Mary Virgin, didst thou wander,
Seeking the beloved Child.
In the Temple thou didst find Him:
O what joy then filled thy heart!
In thy sorrows, in thy gladness,
Grant us, Joseph, to have part.

Clasped in Jesus' arms and Mary's,
When death gently came at last,
Thy pure spirit, sweetly sighing,
From its earthly dwelling passed.
Dear Saint Joseph by that passing,
May our death be like to thine,
And with Jesus, Mary, Joseph,
May our souls forever shine.

St. Basil's Hymnal

O glorious St. Joseph, chosen by God to be the reputed father of Jesus, the most pure spouse of Mary, ever Virgin, and the head of the Holy Family, and then elected by the Vicar of Christ to be the heavenly Patron and Protector of the Church founded by Jesus Christ; with the greatest confidence I implore at this time thy powerful aid for the entire Church militant. Protect in a special manner with thy truly paternal love the Supreme Pontiff and all the Bishops and Priests united to the See of St. Peter. Defend all those who labor for souls in the midst of the afflictions and tribulations of this life, and obtain the willing submission of every nation throughout the world to the Church, the necessary means of salvation for all.

O dearest St. Joseph, be pleased to accept the consecration which I make to thee of myself. I dedicate myself entirely to thee that thou mayest ever be my father, my protector, and my guide in the way of salvation. Obtain for me great purity of heart and a fervent love of the interior life. Grant that after thy example all my actions may be directed to the greater glory of God, in union with the divine Heart of Jesus and the immaculate Heart of Mary, and with thee. Finally, pray for me that I may be able to share in the peace and joy of thy most holy death. Amen.

Grant, O holy Joseph, that, ever secure under thy protection, we may pass our lives without guilt.

Glorious St. Joseph, model of all those who are devoted to labor, obtain for me the grace to work in a spirit of penance for the expiation of my many sins; to work conscientiously, putting the call of duty above my inclinations; to work with gratitude and joy, considering it an honor to employ and develop, by means of labor, the gifts received from God; to work with order, peace, moderation and patience, without ever recoiling before weariness or difficulties; to work, above all, with purity of intention, and with detachment from self, having always death before my eyes and the account which I must render of time lost, of talents wasted, of good omitted, of vain complacency in success, so fatal to the work of God. All for Jesus, all for Mary, all after thy example, O Patriarch Joseph. Such shall be my watchword in life and in death. Amen.

St. Joseph, model and patron of those who love the Sacred Heart of Jesus, pray for us.

DEAR GUARDIAN OF MARY

Dear Guardian of Mary! dear nurse of her Child!
    Life's ways are full weary, the desert is wild;
Bleak sands are all round us, no home can we see;
    Sweet Spouse of our Lady, we lean safe on thee.

For thou to the pilgrim art father and guide,
    And Jesus and Mary felt safe at thy side.
O Glorious Patron, secure shall I be
    Sweet Spouse of our Lady, if thou stay with me.

God chose thee for Jesus and Mary; wilt thou
    Forgive a poor exile for choosing thee now?
There's no Saint in Heaven, St. Joseph like thee,
    Sweet Spouse of our Lady, do thou plead for me.

St. Basil's Hymnal

LITANY OF ST. JOSEPH

Lord, have mercy.
Christ, have mercy.
Lord, have mercy.
Christ, hear us.
Christ, graciously hear us.
God, the Father of Heaven, have mercy on us.
God, the Son, Redeemer of the world, have mercy on us.
God, the Holy Ghost, have mercy on us.
Holy Trinity, one God, have mercy on us.
Holy Mary, pray for us.

St. Joseph,
Renowned offspring of David,
Light of Patriarchs,
Spouse of the Mother of God,
Chaste guardian of the Virgin,
Foster father of the Son of God,
Diligent protector of Christ,
Head of the Holy Family,
Joseph most just,
Joseph most chaste,
Joseph most prudent,
Joseph most strong,
Joseph most obedient,
Joseph most faithful,
Mirror of patience,
Lover of poverty,
Model of artisans,
Glory of home life,
Guardian of virgins,
Pillar of families,
Solace of the wretched,
Hope of the sick,
Patron of the dying,
Terror of demons,
Protector of Holy Church,

Pray for us.

    Lamb of God, Who takest away the sins of the world, spare us, O Lord.

    Lamb of God, Who takest away the sins of the world, graciously hear us, O Lord.

    Lamb of God, Who takest away the sins of the world, have mercy on us.

    V. He made him the lord of His household.

    R. And prince over all His possessions.

Let us pray.

O God, Who in Thy ineffable providence didst vouchsafe to choose blessed Joseph to be the spouse of Thy most holy Mother; grant, we beseech Thee, that we may have him for our intercessor in Heaven, whom we venerate as our protector on earth: Who livest and reignest world without end. Amen.

PRAYER OF ST. MADALEINE SOPHIE BARAT

"Deign to reveal to me, O glorious Saint, the spiritual wealth hidden in a poor and humble life such as thy own life was; obtain for me the interior spirit; vouchsafe to instruct me that I may by thy guidance attain a perfect dependence of myself on the Will of God. Enfold always in the mantle of thy paternal benevolence our society, as thou didst thine own family."

PRAYER OF ST. CLEMENT MARY HOFBAUER

"St. Joseph, my loving father, I place myself forever under thy protection; look on me as thy child, and keep me from all sin. I take refuge in thy arms, so that thou mayest lead me in the path of virtue, and assist me at the hour of my death."

PRAYERS FOR PURITY

O Jesus, Son of the living God, brightness of eternal light, Who from all eternity wast begotten most pure in the bosom of the Eternal Father, and Who in time didst will to be born of a most pure and immaculate Virgin, I, thy creature full of infirmity, beg of Thee, with all my heart, to preserve me pure in mind and body; and do Thou cause to be renewed most abundantly in Thy holy Church the virtue of holy Purity for Thy greater glory and the salvation of the souls Thou hast redeemed.

O most pure and ever-immaculate Virgin Mary, Daughter of the Eternal Father, Mother of the Eternal Son, and Spouse of the Holy Ghost, august and living temple of the Most Adorable Trinity, lily of purity and mirror without stain, obtain for me, dear Mother, I beseech thee, from the good Jesus, purity of mind and body, and beg of Him to cause this beautiful virtue to flourish more and more among all classes of the faithful.

O most chaste Spouse of Mary Immaculate, glorious St. Joseph, who didst merit to receive from God the singular privilege of being the reputed father of Innocence itself, Jesus Christ, and spotless guardian of the Virgin of virgins, obtain for me, I beseech thee, the love of Jesus, my Savior and God, and the special protection of Mary my most blessed Mother; grant, O blessed Joseph, protector of all chaste souls, that this thy beloved virtue of holy purity may be better loved by me and by all men.

And thou who didst so deeply love Jesus, Mary and Joseph, St. Bernardine, my special advocate and example, model of Christian modesty, restorer in our times of piety and holy living, present my prayers, I beseech thee, to the Holy Family, and implore that, together with piety and the fear of God, holy purity of soul and body may reign in all Christian families and in all children of our Mother, the holy Roman Church. Amen.

PRAYER TO ST. JOSEPH FOR PURITY

Guardian of virgins, and holy father Joseph, to whose faithful custody Christ Jesus, Innocence itself, and Mary, Virgin of virgins, were committed; I pray and beseech thee, by these dear pledges, Jesus and Mary, that, being preserved from all uncleanness, I may with spotless mind, pure heart and chaste body, ever serve Jesus and Mary most chastely all the days of my life. Amen.

ST. JOSEPH AND THE DIVINE INFANT

St. Joseph ask thy little Son
    To make me all His own,
That my poor, weak, unstable heart
    May beat for His alone.

How strong in all its ardent love
    Was that pure heart of thine!
It ever beat in unison
    With Jesus' Heart divine.

How oft' upon that heart He slept!
    Nor feared that it would fail —
He knew, dear Saint, the world's weak charms,
    Could n'er o'er thee prevail.

O little Jesus, make my heart
    Like Joseph's heart, all free
From allurements that might draw
    My love, my thoughts, from Thee.

PRAYERS TO THE HOLY FAMILY

Jesus, Mary and Joseph, bless us and grant us the grace to love the Church, as we ought, above every other earthly thing, and always to show forth our love by deeds. Pater, Ave, Gloria.

Jesus, Mary and Joseph, bless us and grant us the grace without fear or human respect openly to profess, as we ought, the faith which was given to us in Baptism. Pater, Ave, Gloria.

Jesus, Mary and Joseph, bless us and grant us the grace to share, as we ought, in the defense and propagation of the Faith, when duty calls, whether by word or by the sacrifice of our fortunes and our lives. Pater, Ave, Gloria.

Jesus, Mary and Joseph, bless us and grant us the grace to love one another, as we ought, and to live together in perfect harmony of thought, will and action, under the rule and guidance of our pastors. Pater, Ave, Gloria.

Jesus, Mary and Joseph, bless us and grant us the grace to conform our lives, as we ought, to the precepts of God and of the Church, so as to live always in that charity which they set forth. Pater, Ave, Gloria.

PRAYER AGAINST BLASPHEMY

To thee we have recourse, St. Joseph, because thou art our protector in our fight against blasphemy. Did thou not, under angelic guidance, give to the Redeemer of the world the holy name of Jesus? Wast thou not the protector of Jesus and Mary? Didst thou not save these two most dear pledges from the sanguinary fury of Herod? And as the Divine Father gave to thee the custody of the house of Nazareth, did not the Supreme Pontiff entrust to thee the Catholic Church in which Jesus now lives and works? See how men blaspheme the Name of God, Our Lady, the Saints, and that which the Church holds most dear, the Blessed Sacrament of the Holy Eucharist in which is Jesus Christ. Stand by us, O great Patriarch, in the war to which we are pledged against this wicked vice, and as the invincible Virgin, by favoring the Christian galleys at Lepanto, overcame the savage Mohammedans, so do thou, O blessed Joseph, help us to drive down to hell, whence it came forth, this blasphemous outcry. Enlighten, dear Saint, the unhappy victims of this sad vice which carries with it the sentence of eternal condemnation, so that being converted they may lament their sin with sincere and heartfelt contrition.

HOLY PATRON, THEE SALUTING

Holy Patron! thee saluting,
Here we meet with hearts sincere;
Blest St. Joseph, all uniting,
Call on thee to hear our pray'r.

Worldly dangers for them fearing,
Youthful hearts to thee we bring,
Grant, in virtue persevering,
Vice may ne'er their bosoms sting.

Happy Saint! in bliss adoring
Jesus, Savior of mankind;
Hear thy children thee imploring,
May we thy protection find.

Thou, who faithfully attended
Him whom heaven and earth adore;
Who with pious care defended
Mary, Virgin ever pure.

May our fervent prayers ascending
Move thee for our souls to plead;
May thy smile of peace descending,
Benedictions on us shed.

Through this life, O watch around us,
Fill with love our every breath,
And when parting fears surround us,
Guide us through the toils of death.

Happy Saint! in bliss adoring
Jesus, Savior of mankind;
Hear thy children thee imploring,
May we thy protection find.
St. Basil's Hymnal.

A PRAYER TO ST. JOSEPH

O Foster Father of Jesus, who taught Him in childhood's hour,
Gentle and tender Joseph, pure spouse of the Virgin Maid!
However the sun be shining, however the skies may lower,
Teach us to follow His teaching, forever, thro' light and shade.

And then when the shadows of evening darkly
    around us hover,
When reason lives no longer, and eyes grow faint
    and dim —
Signs from the Father Almighty that the journey at
    last is over —
Be thou our Guide, O Joseph, and lead us Home
    to Him.

Brian O'Higgins.

PETITIONS TO ST. JOSEPH

Bring to me, my dearest Father,
    Jesus, as my Guest Divine,
In that last eventful hour
    Let His Heart repose in mine.

Pray for me to my sweet Mother,
    That with Jesus she may come
To conduct my soul to Heaven,
    To my true, eternal home.

Dear St. Joseph, oh! remember,
    When thou didst this life depart,
How the blessed Hands of Jesus
    Pillowed thee upon His Heart.

By the grace of thy last moments,
    Dearest Father, pray for me,
That my death be happy, joyous,
    As thy own, mine, too, may be.

Jesus, Mary, Joseph! hear me,
    When your praises I shall sing,
When for favors, graces pleading,
    I to you my sorrows bring.

Oh! refuse not, my last moments,
    With your presence to console,
When to Jesus, Mary, Joseph,
    I resign my heart and soul.

Dear St. Joseph, be thou near me
    When my soul is called away,
From this earth so dark and dreary,
    To the bright, eternal day.

Bring with thee my dearest Jesus,
    In whose wounds I fain would hide,
And with Mary, my dear Mother,
    Come, dear Father, to my side.

    Jesus, Mary, Joseph, I give you my heart and my soul.
    Jesus, Mary, Joseph, assist me in my last agony.
    Jesus, Mary, Joseph, may I breathe forth my soul in peace with you.

THE VISION

Behold the Eternal mid the tools
    Of Joseph's workshop! Yet Time's fools
Scarce recognize Him in that slender Boy.
His white hand pausing in His low employ,
    The shavings awed around His tender feet,
As Heaven opens, and from high let down
    Appears a Cross, in light emblazoned, meet
        For eyes so young and sweet.

    Now dark it looms, and in its frown
    A far, far Vision grows apace

With fear o'er mantling that young face.
O heavy Cross! thy shadow falls upon
    The little shoulders that one day,
Bowed down, shall bear thee o'er a weary way,
Slow-dropping thorns, encrimsoning soil and stone,
      Set in above those heavenly eyes
    Now gazing rapt on Paradise.
O Mary's Boy! her seamless garment gone,
This beauteous Form, disfigured, torn, on high
    Shall there be nailed, for us to die!

Teach us to love Thee, follow Thee, fair Youth,
Who art the perfect Way, the Life, the Truth!
M. S. Pine in "Sacred Poems".

TO ST. JOSEPH

Humblest of men, and honored most,
    Last Patriarch, and most renowned,
Whose name's on every distant coast,
    Whose image in each shrine is found!

Not David, in his royal hour,
    So glorified his kingly line,
As thou, to whose paternal power
    Bowed Mary and her Babe Divine.

Not David's loud, immortal song
    Is as thy silence eloquent.
The glory of his conquests long
    Shall ere thy lowlier fame be spent.

He smote his harp and made it speak
    Down all the corridors of days.
Thou'rt voiceless still, in rapture meek —
    Thy silence fills the world with praise!
Edward F. Garesche, S. J.

ACHIEVEMENT

"Tap-tap" sounds the hammer,
    And "buzz" goes the saw,
As Joseph, the Just Man,
    Fulfills the whole law.

Proud Rome's to the north,
    With her head in the sky,
But God weighs her worth,
    As He passes her by.

And cold, classic Greece
    With her cultured stare,
God heeds her no more
    Than the ambient air.

But this lowly man,
    Toiling hidden from sight,
Is a shaft of pure praise
    Rising white in the night.

"Tap-tap" sounds the hammer,
    And "buzz" goes the saw,
As Joseph, the Just Man,
    Fulfills the whole law.
              C. A. Burns, S. J.

JOSEPH'S GLORIES

What golden goodness shone in thee
    That Mary chose thy bride to be,
And Christ thy foster-child;
    That Angels, forth from Heaven sent,
Woke oft thy love and wonderment,
    Thy grief and care beguiled!

Take heart, ye lowly and ye poor;
    For Joseph's glories more endure
Than wits and counsels keen.
    He from a cottage knew to rise
Above the natives of the skies,
    The consort of their Queen!
John Maryson

ST. JOSEPH

See how my ship is sadly wrecked,
    Smashed on the rocky shore;
The hull I made all by myself
    Can stand the waves no more.

And now I need a carpenter
    To plan and lay the beams,
To teach me how to choose the wood
    And caulk the opened seams.

St. Joseph, will you help me build
    A ship so stout and true
That stormy seas and adverse winds
    Can't wreck this bark anew?

And then, St. Joseph, while I steer,
    Stand by me evermore
Until at last I reach the port
    Where Christ waits on the shore.
Jeanne Norweb

JOSEPH'S THOUGHTS

Jesus' words and Mary's
    Oft the Gospels tell.
Glad we read them over,

>   Pondering them well.
> Sweetness of Heaven
>   In the pages dwell.
>
> Then we gently wonder:
>   "All the pages through
> Never word from Joseph?"
>   Hark, the answer due:
> Jesus' thoughts, and Mary's,
>   They were Joseph's, too.

John Maryson

ON A PICTURE OF ST. JOSEPH

A thin gold circlet frames the sad, tired face
    And patriarchal locks. About the eyes
And mouth, deep lines the story trace
    Of patient suffering and sacrifice.
Yet he has seen his pains and sorrow cease:
    His downcast eyes glow with radiance
Of never-ending joy, infinite peace;
    God's Presence thrills the aged countenance!
For one hand holds the lily-blossomed rod,
    The other proudly thrones the Son of God.

Louis Raymond

HYMN TO ST. JOSEPH

Joseph, our certain hope of life!
    Glory of earth and heaven!
Thou pillar of the world! to thee
    Be praise eternal given.

Thee, as salvation's minister,
    The mighty Maker chose,

As foster father of the Word,
    As Mary's spotless spouse.

With joy thou sawest Him new-born,
    Of Whom the prophets sang;
Him in a manger didst adore,
    From Whom creation sprang.

The Lord of lords, as King of kings,
    Ruler of sky and sea,
Whom heav'n and earth and hell obey,
    Was subject unto thee.

Blest Trinity, vouchsafe to us,
    Through Joseph's merits high,
To mount the heav'nly seats, and reign
    With him eternally. Amen.

TO ST. JOSEPH

Dear St. Joseph, spouse of Mary,
Foster-father of my King,
Take, oh take, this fragrant lily
Which to thee I humbly bring!

I have told the sweet white flower
What I need most for the strife,
Greater courage, much more patience,
Such as thou hadst all through life.

It implores, through thee, the Father,
Grace for me to do God's Will,
As the angels do in Heaven,
And the saints on earth fulfill.

It will tell thee how I love thee,
How I yearn for thy strong aid,

For my soul is sometimes weary,
And, at times, I feel afraid.

Guide my footsteps in this valley,
As thou didst the Sinless One,
On her journey into Egypt,
When she carried Christ, her Son.

Guard me 'gainst the snares of Satan,
Who appears in fond disguise,
And deceives, by words and actions,
Those regarded very wise.

F. deS. Howle, S. J.

COME TO BETHLEHEM

Come to Bethlehem, come and see,
    Him whose birth the angels sing;
Come adore on bended knee,
    Th' Infant Christ, the newborn King.
    Gloria in excelsis Deo.

See within a manger laid,
    Jesus, Lord of heav'n and earth!
Mary, Joseph, lend your aid,
    With us sing our Savior's birth.
    Gloria in excelsis Deo.

VENITE, ADOREMUS

God an infant — born today!
    Born to live, to die, for me!
Bow, my soul: adoring say,
    "Lord, I live, I die, for Thee".
Humble then, but fearless, rise;
Seek the manger where He lies.

Tread with awe the solemn ground
    Tho' a stable mean and rude.
Wondering angels all around
    Throng the seeming solitude:
Swelling anthems, as on high,
Hail a second Trinity.*

'Neath the cavern's** dim-lit shade
    Meekly sleeps a tender form.
God on bed of straw is laid!
    Breaths of cattle keep Him warm!
King of glory, can it be
Thou art thus for love of me?

Hail, my Jesus, Lord of might!
    Here in tiny helpless band
Thy creation's infinite
    Holding like a grain of sand!
Hail, *my* Jesus — all my own:
Mine as if but mine alone!

Hail, my Lady, full of grace!
    Maiden-Mother, hail to thee!
Poring on the radiant face,
    Thine a voiceless ecstasy;
Yet, sweet Mother, let me dare
Join the homage of thy prayer.

Mother of God — O wondrous name!
    Bending Seraphs hail thee queen.
Mother of God, yet still the same
    Mary thou hast ever been:

---

*Jesus, Mary, and Joseph are called the earthly Trinity.
**It was a cavern used as a stable.

Still so lowly, tho' so great —
Mortal, yet Immaculate!

Joseph, hail — of gentlest power!
    Shadow of the Father thou:
Thine to shield in danger's hour
    Whom thy presence comforts now.
Mary trusts to thee her Child;
He His Mother undefiled.

Jesus, Mary, Joseph, hail!
    Saddest year its Christmas brings:
Comes the faith that cannot fail,
    Come the shepherds and the kings:
Gold and myrrh and incense sweet
Come to worship at your feet.

                B. D. Hill, C. S. P., 1876

A MAN OF TREASURE

Three Wise Men came, their gifts to bring
Unto the little new-born King;
Gold, frankincense and myrrh they gave,
Making His crib a treasure-cave.
Happy were they to make Him glad;
Such gifts, they thought, He never had.
They little guessed that Joseph, poor,
Had brought such very gifts before,
A heart of gold, incense of prayer,
And myrrh of all the pains he bare.
Good Wise Men, see a wiser one,
Who calls the God ye worship — Son!

                Rev. Hugh F. Blunt

OUR EPIPHANY

What tho' we cannot, with the star-led kings,
    Adore the swaddled Babe of Bethlehem,
Behold how sweetly Benediction brings
    A new Epiphany denied to them.
The Mary Mystical 'tis ours to see
    Still from His crib the little Jesus take,
And show Him to us on her altar-knee,
    And sing to Him to bless us for her sake.
Shall we the while be kneeling giftless there?
    In loving faith a richer gold shall please;
A costlier incense in the humblest prayer;
    Nor less the myrrh of penitence than these.
And there between us holy priesthood stands,
    Our own Saint Joseph, with the chosen hands.
              B. D. Hill, C. S. P., 1871

A BLESSED MAN

St. Joseph, when you cradled Him
    Within your gentle arm,
And while He softly slumbered on
    Did shelter Him from harm;
I wonder if you ever guessed
    That in His dreaming sleep
He smiled, to think that one day He
    O'er you would vigil keep.

O humble heart, the memories
    Of love God loses not;
Your lullabies that soothed to rest,
    Your care, He ne'er forgot.
O blest reward, when in His arms

You sighed your dying breath!
You cradled Jesus at His birth,
He cradled you at death.
Rev. Hugh F. Blunt

THE RETURN FROM EGYPT

A thousand lights their glory shed
On shrines and altars garlanded;
While swinging censers dusk the air
With perfumed prayer.

And shall we sing the ancestry
Of Jesus, Son of God most high?
Or the heroic names retrace
Of David's race?

Sweeter is lowly Nazareth
Where Jesus drew His childish breath —
Sweeter the singing that endears
His hidden years.

An angel leads the pilgrim band
From Egypt to their native land,
While Jesus clings to Joseph's arm
Secure from harm.

"And the Child grew in wisdom's ken
And years and grace with God and men";
And in His father's humble art
Took share and part.

"With toil", saith He, "My limbs are wet,
Prefiguring the Bloody Sweat";
Ah, how He bears the chastisement
With sweet content!

At Joseph's bench, at Jesus' side,
The Mother sits, the Virgin-Bride,
Happy if she may cheer their hearts
With loving arts.

O Blessed Three, who felt the sting
Of want and toil and suffering,
Pity the needy and obscure
Lot of the poor;

Banish the pride of life from all
Whom ampler wealth and joys befall;
Be every heart with love repaid
That seeks your aid!

Pope Leo XIII (1810-1903)
From the Latin by H. T. Henry

WITH GRATEFUL HEARTS

With grateful hearts we breathe today,
    The tender accents of our love,
We carol forth a little lay
    To thee, great Saint, in Heaven above.

More favored than earth's greatest king,
    Thou wert the guardian of that Child,
Around whose crib full choirs did sing,
    With cadenced voices soft and mild.

All Heaven's host on that great night,
    Looked on the Child, thy Spouse and thee.
And ravished with so far a sight,
    Struck loud their harps with jubilee.

They sang the praises of thy Son,
    In strains of sweetest melody,
And lowly bowed with awe anon,
    Before thy Virgin Spouse and thee.

ST. JOSEPH'S MONTH

Saint of the Childhood and the Hidden Life,
    Why is it that thy month is always Lent?
    What hadst thou with the Passion? Mary went
To Calvary with Jesus; but the knife
Of that fierce sorrow was spared thee. Thy strife
    In anxious care and fostering patience spent:
    Now to a stable, now to Egypt sent,
And then long years with humblest labor rife.
But this thy portion of the coming Cross —
    Which o'er thy path its forward shadow threw.
    And is not ours like thine — to walk content
In that long shadow, counting all things loss
    Save what for Jesus we endure or do? —
    To teach us *this* thy month is always Lent.
                    B. D. Hill, C. S. P., March, 1875

HAIL! HOLY JOSEPH

    Hail! holy Joseph, hail!
        Sweet spouse of Mary, hail!
    Chaste as the lily flower
        In Eden's peaceful vale.

    Hail! holy Joseph, hail!
        Prince of the house of God!
    May His best graces be
        By thy sweet hands bestowed.

    Hail! holy Joseph, hail!
        Comrade of Angels, hail!
    Cheer thou the hearts that faint,
        And guide the steps that fail.

Hail! holy Joseph, hail!
    Teach us our flesh to tame;
And Mary, keep the hearts
    That love Saint Joseph's name.

Hail! holy Joseph, hail!
    Father of Christ esteemed!
Father be thou to those
    Thy Foster-Son redeemed.

Hail! holy Joseph, hail!
    God's choice wert thou alone,
To thee the Word made flesh
    Was subject as a son.

Mother of Jesus, bless,
    And bless, ye Saints on high,
All meek and simple souls
    That to Saint Joseph cry.

Rev. F. W. Faber

SPOUSE OF ST. JOSEPH

Sweet lily-cup
All chaste and pure
So lifted up
That you could lure
The heart of God
To pluck your worth
From out the flowers
Of sinful earth!
Within your chalice
Frail and small
You held the Maker
Of us all!

O Mother dear,
O Lily fair!
Hold fast our lives
Within your care.

    Hilda Laflamme.
Annals of St. Joseph, January, 1954.

PATRON FOR A HAPPY DEATH

To all who would holily live,
To all who would happily die,
St. Joseph is ready to give
Sure guidance, and help from on high.

Of Mary the spouse undefiled,
Just, holy, and pure of all stain,
He asks of his own foster Child,
And needs but to ask to obtain.

In the manger that Child he adored
And nursed Him in exile and flight;
Him, lost in His boyhood, deplored,
And found with amaze and delight.

The Maker of heaven and earth
By the labor of Joseph was fed;
The Son by an infinite birth
Submissive to Joseph was made.

And when his last hour drew nigh,
Oh, full of all joy was his breast,
Seeing Jesus and Mary close by,
As he tranquilly slumbered to rest.

To all who would holily live,
To all who would happily die,
St. Joseph is ready to give
Sure guidance, and help from on high.

DEVOUT INVOCATIONS TO ST. JOSEPH
By Mons. Olier, Founder of St. Sulpice

Hail Joseph, the image of God the Father.

Hail Joseph, foster-father of God the Son.

Hail Joseph, resting place of the Holy Spirit.

Hail Joseph, most faithful assistant of the Great Council.

Hail Joseph, most worthy spouse of the Virgin Mother.

Hail Joseph, guardian of holy virgins.

Hail Joseph, most faithful father of all.

Hail Joseph, great lover of poverty.

Hail Joseph, mirror of humility and obedience.

Hail Joseph, protector of the universal Church.

Hail Joseph, faithful and prudent servant, whom the Lord has placed over His Family.

Blessed are thou among all men.

Blessed are thine ears which have heard what thou hast heard.

Blessed are thine eyes which have seen what thou hast seen.

Blessed are thy hands which have touched the Word made Flesh.

Blessed are thine arms which have borne Him Who bears all things.

Blessed is thy bosom on which the Son of God most sweetly reposed.

Blessed is thy heart inflamed with a most burning love.

And blessed be the Eternal Father, Who chose thee.

Blessed be the Son of God, Who loved thee.

Blessed be the Holy Ghost, Who sanctifed thee.

Blessed be Mary, thy spouse, who loved thee as a spouse and a brother.

Blessed be the Angel who guarded thee.

And blessed forever all who bless thee and love thee.

AN OFFERING TO ST. JOSEPH

O great St. Joseph, thou generous depositary and dispenser of immortal riches, behold us prostrate at thy feet, conjuring thee to receive us as thy servants and as thy children. Next to the Sacred Hearts of Jesus and Mary, of which thou art the faithful copy, we acknowledge that there is no heart more tender, more compassionate than thine.

What, then, have we to fear, or, rather, for what should we not hope, if thou dost deign to be our benefactor, our master, our model, our father, and our mediator? Refuse not, then, this favor, O powerful protector! We ask it of thee by the love thou hast for Jesus and Mary. Into thy hands we commit our souls and bodies, but above all the last moments of our lives.

May we, after having honored, imitated and served thee on earth, eternally sing with thee the mercies of Jesus and Mary. Amen.

AN EFFICACIOUS PRAYER TO ST. JOSEPH

O glorious St. Joseph! faithful follower of Jesus Christ, to thee do we raise our hearts and hands to implore thy powerful intercession in obtaining from the benign Heart of Jesus all the helps and graces necessary for our spiritual and temporal welfare, particularly the grace of a happy death and the special favors we now implore (*mention them.*)

(Then say the following Versicle and Response seven times in honor of the seven Joys and Sorrows of St. Joseph).

V. O glorious St. Joseph, through the love thou bearest to Jesus Christ and for the glory of His Name.

R. Hear our prayers and obtain our petitions.

LET US PRAY

Vouchsafe, O Lord, that we may be helped by the merits of the Spouse of Thy most holy Mother, so that what we cannot obtain of ourselves may be given to us through his intercession. Amen.

NOVENA TO ST. JOSEPH

O glorious St. Joseph, who art that good and faithful servant to whom God committed the care of His Family, whom He appointed guardian and protector of the life of Jesus Christ, the comfort and support of His holy Mother, and instrument in His great design of the Redemption of mankind; thou who hadst the happiness of living with Jesus and Mary, and of dying in their arms; chaste spouse of the Mother of God; model and patron of pure souls; humble, patient and reserved; be moved with the confidence we place in thy intercession; accept with kindness this testimony of our devotion, and procure for us from Almighty God the particular favors which we humbly solicit through thy intercession. (*Ask the favors you wish to obtain*).

We give thanks to God for the signal favors He has been pleased to confer on thee, and we conjure Him, by thy intercession, to make us imitate thy virtues.

With profound humility we entreat thee to be present at the awful hour of our death, when our last grateful words to our Creator shall be "Jesus, Mary, Joseph".

Pray for us, then, O great St. Joseph, and by the love which you hadst for Jesus and Mary, and by the love which Jesus and Mary had for thee, obtain for us the incomparable happiness of living and dying in the love of Jesus and Mary. Amen.

Pater, Ave, Gloria (*which, if time permits, may be repeated seven times in honor of the Seven Joys and Sorrows of St. Joseph*).

PETITIONS FOR ST. JOSEPH'S BLESSING

Bless me, O dearly beloved father, St. Joseph; bless my body and my soul, bless my resolutions, my words and deeds, all my actions and omissions, my every step; bless all that I possess, all my interior and exterior goods, that all may redound to the greater honor of God. Bless me for time and eternity and preserve me from every sin.

Obtain for me the grace to make atonement for all my sins by love and contrition here on earth; so that, after my last breath, I may without delay, prostrate at thy feet, return thee thanks in Heaven for all the love and goodness thou, O dearest father, didst show me here below. Amen.

PRAISES OF ST. JOSEPH

In the name of the Father, and of the Son, and of the Holy Ghost. Amen.

Ever blessed, O holy patriarch, Joseph, be thy soul, which was adorned with all the virtues and gifts of the Holy Ghost.

Glory be to the Father, etc.

Ever blessed, O holy patriarch, Joseph, be thy intellect, which was full of the most sublime knowledge of God and enlightened with revelations.

Glory be to the Father, etc.

Ever blessed, O holy patriarch, Joseph, be thy memory, which always sweetly and fondly remembered Jesus and Mary.

Glory be to the Father, etc.

Ever blessed, O holy patriarch, Joseph, be thy will, which was all inflamed with love for Jesus and Mary, and always perfectly conformable to the Divine Will.

Glory be to the Father, etc.

Ever blessed, O holy Patriarch, Joseph, be thy eyes, to which it was granted to look continually upon Jesus and Mary.

Glory be to the Father, etc.

Ever blessed, O holy patriarch, Joseph, be thy ears, which merited to hear the sweet words of Jesus and Mary.

Glory be to the Father, etc.

Ever blessed, O dear St. Joseph, be thy tongue, which continually praised God, and with profound humility and reverence conversed with Jesus and Mary.

Glory be to the Father, etc.

Ever blessed, O chaste St. Joseph, be thy most pure and love-glowing heart, with which thou didst ardently love Jesus and Mary.

Glory be to the Father, etc.

Ever blessed, O holy Joseph, be thy thoughts, words and actions, each and all of which ever tended to the service of Jesus and Mary.

Glory be to the Father, etc.

Ever blessed, O holy patriarch, Joseph, be all the moments of thy life, which thou didst spend in the service of Jesus and Mary.

Glory be to the Father, etc.

Ever blessed, O my protector, St. Joseph, be that moment of thy life in which thou didst most sweetly die in the arms of Jesus and Mary.

Glory be to the Father, etc.

Ever blessed, O glorious St. Joseph, be that moment in which thou didst enter into the eternal joys of Heaven.

Glory be to the Father, etc.

Ever blessed in eternity, O happy St. Joseph, be every moment in which, until now, in union with all the other saints of Heaven, thou didst enjoy the incomprehensible bliss of union with God, with Jesus and Mary.

Glory be to the Father, etc.

O my dear protector! be thou ever blessed by me and by all creatures, for all eternity, with all the blessings which the Most Holy Trinity bestowed on thee, and with all the benedictions given thee by Jesus and Mary and by the whole Church Triumphant and Militant.

Glory be to the Father, etc.

O thrice holy Joseph, blessed in soul and body, in life and death, on earth and in Heaven, obtain also for me, a poor sinner, but nevertheless thy true and faithful client, a share in thy blessings, the grace to imitate thee ardently, to love and faithfully serve Jesus, Mary and thyself, and especially the happiness to die in thy holy arms.

Glory be to the Father, etc.

* * *

The most effectual devotion we can practise in honor of the Incarnate Word, the Blessed Virgin, and St. Joseph, is:

1. To take as our model of self-contempt the Word in His annihilation, wherein He abased Himself to our miseries by the incomprehensible mystery of the Incarnation.

2. To take as our model of purity the Blessed Virgin, who was so pure in mind and body that she merited that the Son of God, being pleased to become man, should take her for His Mother.

3. To place ourselves under the guidance of St. Joseph, who having been entrusted by God the Father with the direction and control of the exterior actions of His Son, as also of the Blessed Virgin, fulfilled herein an office infinitely more exalted than if he had had the government of all the angels, and the direction of the interior of all the saints.

We ought, then, to address ourselves to him in our functions and employments, and earnestly entreat his guidance, not only in the interior, but also in the exterior life; for it is certain that this great saint has a peculiar power to aid souls in the interior ways, and that we receive much assistance from him in the matter of exterior direction.

Rev. Louis Lallemant, S. J.

Every soul which desires to advance in the interior ways must endeavor to excel in devotion to our Lord and the Holy Spirit, uniting therewith devotion to the Blessed Virgin and St. Joseph, with the hope of attaining humility by the merit of the self-annihilation of the Incarnate Word; purity, by the favor of the Blessed Virgin, the purest of all pure creatures; and the guidance of the Holy Spirit, by the intercession of St. Joseph, for this holy Patriarch having discharged, under the Holy Spirit, the office of governing the Son of God and His holy Mother, by the merit of this charge has acquired, as it were, a kind of right to direct interiorly faithful souls. And, in fact, we have sensible proof that they who take him as their director make wonderful progress under his guidance.

Rev. Louis Lallemant, S. J.

NOVENA TO ST. JOSEPH

by Rev. Louis Lallemant, S. J.

It consists in turning to St. Joseph four times a day (it does not matter when or where) and honoring him in the four points of:

1. His Fidelity to Grace. Think of this for a minute, thank God and ask through St. Joseph to be faithful to grace.
2. His Fidelity to the Interior Life. Think, thank God and and ask.

3. His Love of our Blessed Lady. Think, thank God and ask.
4. His Love of the Holy Child. Think, thank God and ask.
   (Only one point to be taken for each visit.)

EXPLANATION OF THE POINTS TO BE CONSIDERED:

1. FIDELITY TO GRACE — By this is meant St. Joseph's consciousness of sanctifying grace. It also refers to his cooperation with the actual graces that God sent to him constantly, that is, graces which enlightened his mind and moved his will to do good and to avoid evil.

2. FIDELITY TO THE INTERIOR LIFE — The interior life is the life of the soul, the life of grace in the soul, the life of awareness of God and devotion to duty for the honor and glory of God; it embraces also the practice of virtue which is associated with living the interior life, such as the spirit of prayer, the continual remembrance of the presence of God, resignation to God's Will, humility of heart, the spirit of sacrifice and the like.

3. LOVE OF OUR LADY — It means thinking about the devotion of St. Joseph to Mary — how he was chosen by her as her spouse; how he was told by God's messenger of the mystery of her Divine Motherhood. St. Joseph was the protector of Mary and the head of the Holy Family. He realized better than anyone else her part in the Divine Plan for our salvation. His natural love for her was increased and strengthened and perfected by his supernatural love and devotion to her.

4. LOVE OF THE CHRIST CHILD — St. Joseph was told that the Christ Child was the Son of God and the Savior of the world. He was mindful of the duty which was his of protecting and caring for the Infant Savior. His Faith in Christ was manifested in the many trials and difficulties that

St. Joseph experienced. His love for Jesus was deep and genuine and profound. It was a love that revealed itself not only in word, but especially in service.

CHAPLET IN HONOR OF THE SEVEN SORROWS AND SEVEN JOYS OF ST. JOSEPH

1. Pure spouse of most holy Mary, glorious St. Joseph, the travail and anguish of thy heart were great, when, being in sore perplexity, thou wast minded to put away thy stainless spouse; yet wast thy joy inexpressible when the Archangel revealed to thee the sublime mystery of the Incarnation.

By this, thy sorrow and thy joy, we pray thee comfort our souls now and in their last pain with the consolation of a well spent life, and holy death, like unto thine own, with Jesus and Mary at our side.

Our Father, Hail Mary, Glory be.

2. Most blessed Patriarch, glorious St. Joseph, chosen to the office of reputed father of the Word made Man, the pain was keen when thou didst see the Infant Jesus born in abject poverty; but thy pain was changed into heavenly joy when thou didst hear the harmony of Angel choirs, and beheld the glory of that night.

By this, thy sorrow and thy joy, we pray thee, obtain for us that, when the journey of life is over, we too may pass to that blessed land where we shall hear the Angel chants, and rejoice in the bright light of heavenly glory.

Our Father, Hail Mary, Glory be.

3. O thou who wast ever most obedient in executing the commands of God, glorious St. Joseph, thy heart wast pierced with pain when the blood of the precious Infant

Savior was shed at His circumcision; but the Name of Jesus brought thee new life and heavenly joy.

By this, thy sorrow and thy joy, obtain for us that, being freed in this life from every vice, we too may cheerfully die with the sweet Name of Jesus in our hearts and on our lips.

Our Father, Hail Mary, Glory be.

4. Most faithful Saint, glorious St. Joseph, who wast admitted to take part in the Redemption of man, the prophecy of Simeon foretelling the sufferings of Jesus and Mary caused thee a pang like that of death but, at the same time, this prediction of the salvation and glorious resurrection of innumerable souls filled thee with great joy.

By this, thy sorrow and thy joy, help us with thy prayers to be of the number of those who, through the merits of Jesus and the intercession of His Virgin Mother, shall be partakers of the resurrection to glory.

Our Father, Hail Mary, Glory be.

5. Most watchful guardian and bosom friend of the Incarnate Son of God, glorious St. Joseph, how greatly didst thou toil to nourish and to serve the Son of the Most High, especially in the flight thou didst make with Him into Egypt, thou didst also greatly rejoice to have God Himself forever with thee and to see the overthrow of the idols of Egypt.

By this, thy sorrow and thy joy, obtain for us grace to keep far out of the reach of the enemy of our souls, by quitting all dangerous occasions, so that no idol of earthly affection may any longer occupy our hearts, but that being entirely devoted to the service of Jesus and Mary, we may live and die for them alone.

Our Father, Hail Mary, Glory be.

6. Angel on earth, glorious St. Joseph, who didst marvel to see the King of Heaven obedient to thy bidding, even if the consolation of thy heart on bearing Him home was disturbed by the fear of Archelaus, nevertheless, being reassured by the Angel, thou didst go back and dwell happily at Nazareth, in the company of Jesus and Mary.

By this, thy sorrow and thy joy, obtain for us that, having our heart free from idle fears, we may enjoy the peace of a tranquil conscience, dwelling safely with Jesus and Mary and dying at last in their arms.

Our Father, Hail Mary, Glory be.

7. Example of holy living, glorious St. Joseph, when through no fault of thine thou didst lose Jesus, the Holy Child, thou didst seek Him with great sorrow for three days, until with unspeakable joy, thou didst find Him, Who was thy Life, amidst the doctors in the Temple.

By this, thy sorrow and thy joy, we beg thee with our whole hearts to intercede in our behalf so that we may never lose Jesus by mortal sin, but if we are at any time so wretched as to lose Him, we will seek Him with unwearied sorrow until we find Him, particularly at the hour of our death, so that we may pass from this life to enjoy Him forever in Heaven, there to sing with thee His divine mercies without end.

Our Father, Hail Mary, Glory be.

LET US PRAY

O God, Who in Thine ineffable providence didst vouchsafe to choose blessed Joseph to be the spouse of Thy most holy Mother, grant, we beseech Thee, that we may be worthy to have him for our intercessor in Heaven, whom on earth we venerate as our protector. Who livest and reignest world without end. Amen.

THIRTY DAYS' PRAYER TO ST. JOSEPH

Ever blessed and glorious Joseph, kind and indulgent father, and compassionate friend of all in sorrow, through that bitter grief with which thy heart was saturated when thou didst behold the sufferings of the Infant Savior, and in prophetic view didst contemplate His most ignominious Passion and Death, take pity, I beseech thee, on my poverty and necessities, counsel me in my doubts, and console me in all my anxieties.

Thou art the good father and protector of orphans, the advocate of the defenseless, the patron of those who are in need and desolation. Do not, then, disregard the petition of thy poor child. My sins have drawn down upon me the just displeasure of my God, and hence I am surrounded with sorrows. To thee, O loving guardian of the poor neglected Family of Nazareth, do I fly for shelter and protection.

Listen, then. I entreat thee, with a father's solicitude to the earnest prayer of thy poor suppliant and obtain for me the object of my petition. I ask it by that infinite mercy of the eternal Son of God which induced Him to assume our nature, and to be born into this world of sorrow. I ask it by that grief which filled thy heart when ignorant of the mystery wrought in thy Immaculate Spouse thou didst fear thou shouldst be separated from her.

I ask it by that weariness, solicitude and suffering which thou didst endure when thou soughtest in vain at the inns of Bethlehem a shelter for the Holy Virgin and a birthplace for the Infant God, and when, being everywhere refused, thou wert obliged to consent that the Queen of Heaven should give birth to the world's Redeemer in a wretched stable.

I ask it by the painful blood-shedding thou didst witness at His Circumcision. I ask it by the sweetness and power of that sacred Name, Jesus, which thou didst confer on the adorable Infant. I ask it by that mortal anguish inflicted on thee by the prophecy of holy Simeon which declared the Child Jesus and His Holy Mother to be the future victims of their own great love for us and for our sins.

I ask it through that sorrow and anguish which filled thy soul when the Angel declared to thee that the life of the Child Jesus was sought for by His enemies, from whose impious design thou wert obliged to fly with Him and His Blessed Mother into Egypt.

I ask it by all the pains, fatigues and toils of that long and perilous journey. I ask it by all the sorrows thou didst endure when in Egypt, when sometimes thou wert not able, even by the sweat of thy brow, to procure daily food for thy poor family.

I ask it by all thy solicitude to preserve the Sacred Child and His Immaculate Mother during the second journey, when thou wert ordered to return to thy native country. I ask it by thy peaceful dwelling in Nazareth, in which so many joys and sorrows were mingled.

I ask it by thy extreme affliction in being three days deprived of the company of the adorable Child. I ask it by thy joy at finding Him in the Temple, and by the unspeakable consolation imparted to thee in the cottage of Nazareth while living in the society of Jesus. I ask it by that wonderful condescension by which He submitted Himself to thy will.

I ask it through that sorrowful foresight we may believe thee to have had continually in thy mind of all the Infant Jesus was to suffer, when thou shouldst be no longer by His side. I ask it by that painful contemplation by which we may believe thou didst foresee those Divine Infant Hands and Feet, now so active in serving thee, one day pierced with cruel nails; that Head which rested gently on thy breast, crowned with sharp thorns; that delicate Body which thou didst tenderly fold in thy mantle and press to thy heart, stripped, mangled, and extended on a Cross.

I ask it by that perfect love and conformity with which thou didst receive the Divine order to depart from this life and from the company of Jesus and Mary. I ask it by that exceeding great joy which filled thy soul when the Redeemer of the world, triumphant over death and hell, entered into possession of His Kingdom, and conducted thee also into it with special honors. I ask it through Mary's glorious Assumption, and through that endless bliss which with her thou wilt eternally derive from the presence of God.

O good father! I beseech thee, by all thy sufferings, sorrows and joys, to hear me and obtain the grant of my earnest petitions. — (*Here name them or reflect on them.*)

Obtain for all those who have asked my prayers all that is useful to them in the designs of God. And finally, my dear patron and father, be thou with me and all who are dear to me in our last moments, that we may eternally chant the praises of Jesus, Mary and Joseph in Heaven. Amen.

Daughters of St. Paul

IN MASSACHUSETTS
  50 St. Paul's Ave. Jamaica Plain, Boston, MA 02130;
    617-522-8911; 617-522-0875;
  172 Tremont Street, Boston, MA 02111; **617-426-5464;**
    617-426-4230
IN NEW YORK
  78 Fort Place, Staten Island, NY 10301; **212-447-5071**
  59 East 43rd Street, New York, NY 10017; **212-986-7580**
  7 State Street, New York, NY 10004; **212-447-5071**
  625 East 187th Street, Bronx, NY 10458; **212-584-0440**
  525 Main Street, Buffalo, NY 14203; **716-847-6044**
IN NEW JERSEY
  Hudson Mall — Route 440 and Communipaw Ave.,
    Jersey City, NJ 07304; **201-433-7740**
IN CONNECTICUT
  202 Fairfield Ave., Bridgeport, CT 06604; **203-335-9913**
IN OHIO
  2105 Ontario St. (at Prospect Ave.), Cleveland, OH 44115; **216-621-9427**
  25 E. Eighth Street, Cincinnati, OH 45202; **513-721-4838**
IN PENNSYLVANIA
  1719 Chestnut Street, Philadelphia, PA 19103; **215-568-2638**
IN FLORIDA
  2700 Biscayne Blvd., Miami, FL 33137; **305-573-1618**
IN LOUISIANA
  4403 Veterans Memorial Blvd., Metairie, LA 70002; **504-887-7631;**
    504-887-0113
  1800 South Acadian Thruway, P.O. Box 2028, Baton Rouge, LA 70821
    504-343-4057; 504-343-3814
IN MISSOURI
  1001 Pine Street (at North 10th), St. Louis, MO 63101; **314-621-0346;**
    314-231-5522
IN ILLINOIS
  172 North Michigan Ave., Chicago, IL 60601; **312-346-4228**
IN TEXAS
  114 Main Plaza, San Antonio, TX 78205; **512-224-8101**
IN CALIFORNIA
  1570 Fifth Avenue, San Diego, CA 92101; **714-232-1442**
  46 Geary Street, San Francisco, CA 94108; **415-781-5180**
IN HAWAII
  1143 Bishop Street, Honolulu, HI 96813; **808-521-2731**
IN ALASKA
  750 West 5th Avenue, Anchorage AK 99501; **907-272-8183**
IN CANADA
  3022 Dufferin Street, Toronto 395, Ontario, Canada
IN ENGLAND
  57, Kensington Church Street, London W. 8, England
IN AUSTRALIA
  58 Abbotsford Rd., Homebush, N.S.W., Sydney 2140, Australia